D1298162

Jane's
POCKET GUIDE

ADVANCED TACTICAL FIGHTERS

In the USA for information address:
HarperCollinsPublishers Inc.
10 East 53rd Street
New York
NY 10022

In the UK for information address:
HarperCollinsPublishers
77-85 Fulham Palace Road
Hammersmith
London W6 8JB

First Published in Great Britain by HarperCollinsPublishers 1998

1 3 5 7 9 10 8 6 4 2

© HarperCollinsPublishers 1998

ISBN 0 00 472135 7

Design: Rod Teasdale

Colour reproduction by Colorscan
Printed in Italy

Jane's
POCKET GUIDE
ADVANCED
TACTICAL
FIGHTERS

JEREMY FLACK

HarperCollins*Publishers*

Contents

Contents

Introduction

The development of modern fighter aircraft represents an astonishing leap in technology within the space of a single lifetime. Rifles and guns can be traced back to black powder weapons of the 14th century, while the warships date back at least 3,000 years. But the history of powered aircraft only dates from 1903, when the Wright brothers made their historic first flight.

During World War I, the first fighters were no more than reconnaissance aircraft with a precariously mounted machine-gun. The Fokker Eindekker was the first real fighter, fitted with interrupter gear so that its gun could fire through the propeller blades. War provided the impetus for aircraft performance to improve rapidly until 1918, but it was a civilian competition that stimulated another burst of progress. When the Supermarine S.6B won the coveted Schneider Cup in 1931, it did so by achieving a speed of 340.08 mph: about 140 mph faster than military aircraft then in service.

In Britain, R J Mitchell developed the S.6B into the Spitfire, while Hawker developed the Hurricane. In Germany, the Messerschmitt Bf 109 was entering service in a fanfare of publicity. When World War II broke out it was these three aircraft that saw most of the early action. Of course there were a large number of other types and fighter performance improved rapidly. By 1939 fighter top speeds were in the region of 300 mph, but many of the older biplanes sill in front line service were at least 50 mph slower. By the end of the war maximum speeds had increased to around 450 mph–about as fast as propeller-driven aircraft could go.

During the late 1930s, British and German designers began to experiment with jet engines. Initial flight tests proved the practicality of the designs but power-to-weight ratios were still marginal. As the tide of war turned against Germany, the *Luftwaffe* resorted to this immature technology, getting its early jets into battle before the British. The first all-jet air battle took place in 1950 over Korea when a formation of Russian MiG-15s confronted a smaller number of American P-80 fighter-bombers: one of the MiG-15s was shot down.

By the beginning of the 1950s fighter speeds were approaching 700 mph, but this was soon to change. Lockheed interviewed USAF veterans from Korea and incorporated their ideas and requirements in a radical new fighter. The F-104 Starfighter, first flown in 1954 was designed to be capable of Mach 2+ from the outset. Always a controversial aircraft, the Starfighter still remains in service with several countries at the end of the century. Around the rest of the world new fighters were being developed but with a little more modest speed in the Mach 1+ range. By the early 1960s some of today's familiar names had appeared.

The McDonnell Douglas F-4 Phantom became a major player with its multi-role capability, a feature that was beginning to appear due to the spiralling cost of acquiring the latest technology. The Draken, Mirage, MiG-21 and F-5 all emerged about this time and still remain in service, although as later production models. Some have been the subject of comprehensive upgrades to extend their service lives; others will be soon be withdrawn.

By the next decade fighter speed had reached a maximum with the MiG-25 and F-15 Eagle exceeding Mach 2.5 and the YF-12A aircraft reached Mach 3. The days of the pure fighter had also reached a high point

with the development costs now reaching astronomic sums. The multi-role approach had become the rule rather than the exception. New avionics systems, able to locate potentially hostile aircraft at ever increasing ranges have had a profound impact, with beyond visual range (BVR) engagements possible at over 100 miles. The very latest technology is 'stealth' which renders the aircraft virtually invisible on radar.

In this book I describe all currently serving types of aircraft that have a major fighter role. Some are close to being withdrawn from service, while others are in their prime. I have also included a few that are in project stage, and represent a taste of what may be seen in the near future.

If, like the Iraqi air force you are unable to see the Stealth Fighter, don't worry. I have not included it. Although it has the F-117 USAF fighter designation, this aircraft, like the famous F-111 before it, is actually a bomber. It will be included in one of the next titles in this series.

Jeremy Flack

CAC J-7 NATO reporting name 'Fishbed' (China)

Type: Single-seat fighter and close support aircraft.

Development/History

The CAC J-7 (Jianjiji-7 or Fighter Aircraft-7, usually referred to as the F-7 by western nations) is the result of a license granted in 1961 by the Soviet Union for the Chinese to build the MiG-21F. Pattern aircraft and unassembled kits were supplied, but with incomplete documentation. Nevertheless, by 1964 the first J-7 was being assembled by Shenyang using Chinese manufactured components. With static testing complete the first Shenyang J-7 took to the air on 17 January 1966. In 1982, GAIC began the design of the two-seat trainer variant Jianjiji Jiaolianji-7 (JJ-7 or FT-7) and this took to the air for the first time on 5 July 1985.

Production of the J-7 proceeded with some 600 aircraft being delivered to the air force of the Peoples' Liberation Army. In addition, export models have resulted in approximately 1000 J-7s being built.

Variants

J-7: Prototype
J-7 I: Initial production model with front hinged canopy.
F-7A: Export model of J-7 I.
J-7 II: Re-engined J-7 I plus other internal improvements. Brake chute relocated to base of rudder.
F-7B: Export model of J-7 II with R.550 Magic AAM capability.
F-7BS: Hybrid F-7B fuselage and tail plus F-7M wings and basic avionics.
F-7E: Upgraded J-7 II with modified double-delta wing.
F-7M Airguard: Upgraded export model of J-7 II (See separate entry).
JJ-7/FT-7: Two-seat operational trainer.

Specification of J-7 III

Powerplant
1 x LMC WP13 turbojet.
Power: 40.2 kN (9,040 lb st) dry, 64.7 kN (14,550 lb) with afterburner.

Dimensions
Length: 14.885 m (48 ft 10 ins) including probe
Span: 8.32 m (27 ft 3 1/2 ins)
Height: 4.105 m (13 ft 5 1/2 ins)

Weights
Empty: 5,275 kg (11,629 lb)
Max T/O: 8,150 kg (17,967 lb)

Performance
Max Speed: Mach 2.10 at altitude.
Range: 960 km (596 miles) internal fuel only.

Armament
1 x twin barrel 23 mm cannon plus five external attachment points. Typical load is one PL-2/2A, PL-5B, PL-7 or R.550 Magic, plus a drop tank under each wing and a drop tank on the centreline pylon. Alternatively a range of AGM missiles, rocket pods or bombs can be carried.

A Chinese PL-2A AAM fitted to the FT-7. The PL-2A is a licence built model of the Russian R-13 (AA-2 'Atoll') AAM. (Jeremy Flack)

Status
Production complete

Customers
Albania (F-7A), China (J-7 I/II/III/E), Egypt (F-7B), Iraq (F-7B), Sri Lanka (F-7BS), Sudan (F-7B), Tanzania (F-7A),

Manufacturer
CAC (Chengdu Aircraft Corporation) - China

The FT-7 is the two seat model of the J-7/F-7 fighter.

(Jeremy Flack)

CAC F-7M Airguard (China)

Type: Single seat fighter and close support aircraft.

Development/History

The F-7M Airguard is an upgraded variant of the J-7 II which was developed in the late 1970s for export. Incorporated in this model are western avionics including a GEC Marconi Head Up Display (HUD) and weapon aiming computer. Other improvements include a new ranging radar, a more secure radio, and improved engine as well as the ability to carry the improved PL-7 air-to-air missile.

A recognition feature of the F-7M is the nose probe which has been relocated offset at the top of the air intake rather than under it. Note, this is also a feature of the J-7 III which also has a modified wing shape.

Variants

F-7M: Basic production model.
F-7MG: Improved F-7M with F-7E wing together with avionics and engine improvements.
F-7PG: Proposed development - no further details known.
F-7P: (also referred to as Skyguard). Incorporates modifications specific to Pakistan air force requirements including ability to carry up to 4 x Sidewinder AAM and fitting of Martin Baker ejector seat.
F-7MP: The F-7P with additional modifications including improved cockpit layout and navigation aids and fire control.
Super-7: Proposed development of the F-7M with Grumman but subsequently abandoned.

Specification

The Chinese PL-5B AAM   *(Jeremy Flack)*

Powerplant

1 x Chengdu WP7B(BM) turbojet
Power: 43.2 kN (9,700 lb st) dry, 59.82 kN (13,448 lb st) with afterburning.

Dimensions

Length: 14.885 m (48 ft 10 ins) including probe
Span: 7.15 m   (23 ft 5 5/8 ins)
Height: 4.105m (13 ft 5 1/2 ins)

Weights

Empty: 5,275 kg (11,629 lb)
Max T/O: 7,531 kg (16,603 lb)

Performance

Max Speed: 2,175 km/h (1,350 mph)
Range: 960 km (596 miles) internal fuel only

Armament

2 x 30 mm cannon plus five external attachment points capable of carrying PL-2, PL-2A PL-5B, PL-7 air-to-air missiles (or R.550 Magic as a customers option), rocket pods or 1,300 kg of bombs.

Status

Production complete.

Customers

Bangladesh, Iran, Burma, Pakistan (F-7P & F-7MP) and Zimbabwe

Manufacturer

Xian - China
CAC (Chengdu Aircraft Corporation) - China

The Shenyang F-7M armed with rocket pods, AAMs and fitted with a drop tank.

(CAC via API)

CAC FC-1 (China)

Type: Single-seat air superiority fighter and ground attack fighter

Development/History

The programme to build the Fighter China (FC) commenced in 1991 following the US withdrawal from the CAC Super-7 project. With assistance from the MAPO OKB a pair of static test airframes were built and entered a test phase in 1996. Three prototypes have been built and it is expected that the first FC-1 will enter service around the year 2000.

The FC-1 has been designed as a replacement for the Shenyang J-6, CAC J-7 and the Nanchang Q-5 as well as the Western Northrop F-5 and Mirage III/5. Initial orders are expected for the air force of the People's Liberation Army (Chinese air force) and Pakistan air force.

Variants

None at present

Specification

Powerplant

1 x Klimov RD-93 turbofan
Power: 81.4 kN (18,300 lb st) with afterburning.

Dimensions

Length: 13.95 m (45 ft 9 1/4 ins)
Span: 9.50 m (31 ft 2 ins) (including wingtip missiles
Height: 13.95 m (45 ft 9 1/4 ins)

Weights

Empty: 9,300 kg (20,530 lb)
Max T/O: 12,500 kg (27,557 lb)

Performance

Max Speed: Mach 1.6 to 1.8 at altitude
Range: 1,600 km (994 miles)

Armament

Seven external attachment points for total of 3,600 kg (7,937 lb) of stores. Typically a 23 mm twin barrel cannon pod on the centreline plus a PL-7 AAM on each wingtip and a further PL-10 under each wing plus a pair of drop tanks. Alternative loads can include a range of AGMs, bombs, rocket pods and drop tanks.

Status

In development

Manufacturer

CAC (Chengdu Aircraft Corporation) - China

NAMC Q-5 NATO reporting name 'Fantan' (China)

Type: Single-seat close support and ground attack aircraft with air-to-air combat capability

Development/History

The Qiangjiji-5 was derived from the J-6 fighter, which was itself based on the reverse-engineered MiG-19. Designed by Shenyang, the Q-5 has a large radar fitted in the nose that required the air intakes to be positioned either side of the cockpit. The Q-5 prototype first took to the air on 4 June 1965. Approximately 1,000 of all variants of the Q-5 have been built. It is basically an attack aircraft but it is capable of carrying a wide range of air-to-air missiles. These include western as well as Chinese-built missiles.

Variants

Q-5: Initial production variant with internal weapons bay.

Q-5 I: Weapons bay used for additional fuel but external stores points increased from four to eight.

Q-5 IA: Additional two external stores points plus EW/ECM.

Q-5 II: Similar to Q-5 IA with RWR.

Q-5 III: See A-5C.

Q-5K: Proposed upgrade with French avionics not proceeded with.

A-5C: Export variant of modified Q-5 I also referred to as Q-5 III.

A-5M: Upgraded Q-5 II in conjunction with Aeritalia/Alenia of Italy. Fitted with improved radar and nav/attack system.

The A-5C appeared at the Paris Air Show in 1987.

Specification for A-5C

Powerplant
2 x Liming WP6 turbojets
Power: 25.5 kN (5,730 lb st) dry, 31.9 kN
(7,165 lb st) with afterburning.

Dimensions
Length: 16.77 m (55 ft 0 1/4 ins) including probe
Span: 9.70 m (31 ft 10 ins)
Height: 4.515 m (14 ft 9 3/4 ins)

Weights
Empty: 6,638 kg (14,634 lb)
Max T/O: 12,000 kg (26,455 lb)

The A-5C armed with rocket pods and bomb plus fitted with drop tanks.

(Jeremy Flack)

Performance
Max Speed: Mach 1.12 at altitude
Range: 1,820 km ((1,130 miles)

Armament
2 x 23 mm cannons plus 10 external attachment
points capable of a total of 2,505 kg. A wide range
of weapons can be carried ranging from Chinese PL-
2 and PL-7 AAMs and Western AIM-9 Sidewinder
and R.550 Magic AAMs through to rockets and
bombs of various types and drop tanks.

Status
Production complete

Customers
Bangladesh, (A-5C), North Korea (Q-5 I), Burma (A-
5C), Pakistan (A-5C III)

Manufacturer
NAMC (Nanchang Aircraft Manufacturing Company)
- China

The improved A-5M displays a mixed load of French R.550 Magic AAMs plus Chinese rocket pods, bombs and drop tanks.

(Shenyang via API)

Shenyang J-6 NATO reporting name 'Farmer' (China)

Type: Single-seat day interceptor and air superiority fighter.

Development/History

The J-6 (Jainjiji-6 or Fighter Aircraft 6, referred to in the west as the F-6) is a Chinese built MiG-19 'Farmer'. In Russia the MiG-19 production came to an end towards the end of the 1950s. Built in large numbers, these aircraft found their way to most nations in the Warsaw Pact and most countries supported by the Soviet bloc. China however, had only received modest quantities before a political split between the USSR and China halted deliveries. In urgent need of a modern fighter, the Chinese reverse-engineered the MiG-19 and put it into production themselves. The first J-6 took to the air in December 1961 and since then some 3,500 are thought to have been built for the air force of the People's Liberation Army and navy. Although built for air defence, the J-6 fulfils various roles including close air support and reconnaissance.

The J-6 competed for export sales with the Soviet-built MiG-19. Although the design was old, the airframes were new and the Chinese-built model saw a substantial success in the world market.

Variants

J-6: 'Farmer-C' Chinese equivalent of MiG-19S/SF.
J-6A: 'Farmer-D' Chinese equivalent of MiG-19PF with gun and rocket armament.
J-6B: 'Farmer-D' Chinese equivalent of MiG-19PM armed with AA-1 'Alkali' AAM.
J-6C: Development of J-6 recognisable by brake chute re-located in bullet faring at base of rudder.
J-6X: Upgraded model J-6A with Chinese built radar.

Specification J-6 'Farmer-C'

Powerplant
2 x Shenyang built Wopen 6 (WP-6) turbojet developed from Turmansky R-9BF-811.
Power: 25.5 kN (5,732 lb st) dry, 31.8 kN (7,167 lb st) with afterburner.

Dimensions
Length: 14.9 m (48 ft 10 1/2 ins) including probe.
Span: 9.20 m (30 ft 2 1/4 ins)
Height: 3.88 m (12 ft 8 3/4 ins)

Weights
Empty: 5,760 kg (12,700 lb)
Max T/O: 10,000 kg (22,000 lb)

Performance
Max Speed: 1,540 km/h (957 mph) at altitude.
Range: 2,200 miles (1,366 miles) with 2 drop tanks.

Armament
2 or 3 x 30 mm cannon plus six external attachment points. Typical load is an AAM on the outer position on either wing, drop tank on the middle and a further AAM on the inner position. Alternatively, other missiles, bombs or rocket pods can be carried.

Status
Production complete

Customers
Albania, Bangladesh, China, Egypt, Iran, Kampuchea, Pakistan, Tanzania, Vietnam, Zimbabwe.

Manufacturer
Shenyang - China

JJ-6: Two-seat trainer model.
FT-6: Westernised designation of JJ-6.
JZ-6: Fighter/reconnaissance model similar to MiG-19R.
J-6 III: Proposed J-6 with reduced wing span and wing-tip AAMs and ranging radar. Reported to have been capable of Mach 1.48.

A Shenyang F-6 of the Pakistani air force.

(Lindsay Peacock)

Shenyang J-8 NATO reporting name 'Finback' (China)

Type: Single-seat, air-superiority fighter with secondary capability for ground attack.

Development/History

Development of the J-8 commenced in 1964 with the first prototype taking to the air on 5 July 1969. The production go-ahead was given in the same year and continued until 1987. The first flight of the much improved J-8 II took place on 12 June 1984. This variant differs from the previous models in that the single nose intake was split and repositioned on either side of the fuselage just aft of the cockpit. This enabled a new fire control radar and improved avionics to be housed in the now solid nose.

Variants

J-8: 'Finback-A' Clear weather day fighter with provision for up to four wing mounted PL-2B AAMs and a ranging radar in the nose centre body.

J-8 I: 'Finback-A' All weather model, fitted with improved SR-4 fire control radar in the nose centre body. 30 mm cannon replaced by 23 mm cannon.

J-8 II: 'Finback-B' All weather dual-role model (high-altitude interceptor and ground-attack) incorporating some 70 per cent re-design. Intake moved and enlarged giving greater air flown to the more powerful WP13A engines.

F-8 II: Export model with 4 per cent uprated engines. Incorporated Doppler radar and other avionic improvements together with in-flight refuelling and 7 external stores stations for up to 4,500 kg load.

F-8 IIM: Further upgrade to F-8 II (see separate entry)

Specification for J-8 II

Powerplant
2 x Liyang WP13A II turbojets.
Power: 42.7 kN (9,590 lb st) dry, 65.9 kN (14,815 lb st) with afterburning.

Dimensions
Length: 21.59 m (70 ft 10 ins) including probe.
Span: 9.345 m (30 ft 8 ins)
Height: 5.41 m (17 ft 9 ins)

Weights
Empty: 9,820 kg (21,649 lb)
Max T/O: 17,800 kg (39,242 lb)

Performance
Max Speed: 1,300 km/h (808 mph)
Range: 800 km (497 miles)

Armament
1 x 23 mm twin-barrel cannon + 7 external stores stations that can carry a mixture of PL-2B or PL-7 AAMs, rocket pods or bombs with drop tanks on the outer and centre-line stores stations only.

Status
Production complete.

Customers
China

Manufacturer
Shenyang Aircraft Corporation (SAC) - China

The Shenyang F-8 II armed with rocket pods, AAMs and bombs. *(Jeremy Flack)*

Close up of the AAMs on the F-8 II. *(Jeremy Flack)*

Shenyang J-8 IIM NATO reporting name 'Finback' (China)

Type: Single-seat air superiority fighter with secondary capability for ground attack

Development/History

The J-8 IIM is the latest variant of the J-8 family. It evolved following the break down of the 'Peace Pearl' programme in which it was proposed to upgrade the J-8 II with Western avionics. This was embargoed by the US government in 1989 after the massacre of protesters in Beijing, and cancelled by China in 1990. However, the F-8 IIM has been fitted with a number of Russian avionics and has the capability to carry the export versions of the Vympel R-77 (Adder) and Spetztekhnia (R-27R (Alamo) missiles. The first flight of the J-8 IIM was made on 31 March 1996.

Specification

Powerplant
2 x Liyang WP13B turbojet.
Power: 47.1 kN (10,582 lb st) dry, 68.7 kN (15,432 lb st) with afterburner.

Dimensions
Length: 21.59 m (70 ft 10 ins) including probe.
Span: 9.345 m (30 ft 8 ins)
Height: 5.41 m (17 ft 9 ins)

Weights
Empty: 10,371 kg (22,864 lb)
Max T/O: 18,879 kg (41,621 lb)

Performance
Max Speed: Mach 2.2 at altitude.
Range: 1,900 km (1,180 miles) ferry range.

Armament
1 x 23 mm cannon plus five external attachment points. AAMs that can be carried include PL-9, R-77 (AA-12 'Adder') and R-27R1 (AA-10 'Alamo')

Status
In development

Customers
None

Manufacturer
Shenyang Aircraft Corporation (SAC) - China

The Shenyang J-8 IIM.
(Shenyang via API)

Dassault Mirage III (France)

Type: Single-seat interceptor, ground attack or reconnaissance aircraft.

Development/History

The Mirage III was the Dassault proposal for a small supersonic interceptor. The French air force specified that this would require a combination of jet and rocket power, but Dassault decided that this would be too restrictive and proceeded with their own design as a private venture. The prototype was first flown in November 1956 and the French air force were quick to take notice. An order was placed for 10 pre-production aircraft. A production order for the IIIC soon followed and the Mirage family became firmly established.

Dassault incorporated a tough undercarriage in order that the Mirage could operate from rough front-line airstrips, but the delta design requires a high landing speed and this was not practical.

Specification of Mirage IIIE

Powerplant
1 x SNECMA Atar 9C turbojet.
Power: 41.9kN (9,430 lb st) dry, 60.8 kN (13,670 lb st) with afterburner.

Dimensions
Length: 15.03 m (49 ft 3 1/2 ins)
Span: 8.22 m (27 ft 0 ins)
Height: 4.25 m (13 ft 11 1/2 ins)

Weights
Empty: 7.050 kg (15,540 lb)
Max T/O: 13,500 kg (29,760 lb)

Performance
Max Speed: Mach 2.2 at altitude.
Range: 2,400 km (1,492 miles)

Armament
2 x 30 mm cannons plus three external stores locations. Typical load is one R.530 AAM under the fuselage and one Sidewinder or Magic AAM plus a drop tank under each wing. Alternatively, a range of AGMs, bombs or rocket pods can be fitted.

Status
Production completed.

Customers
Argentine (EA), Australia (D/O), Brazil (EBR), France (A/B/BE/E/R/RD), Lebanon (EL), Pakistan (EP), South Africa (EZ), Spain (DE/EE), Switzerland (BS/DS/RS/S), Venezuela (EV)

Manufacturer
Dassault - France
Government Aircraft Factories - Australia
Federal Aircraft Factory - Switzerland

French air force Mirage IIIC of EC2/10 armed with the Matra R.530 AAM. (Jeremy Flack)

Dassault Mirage III (France)

Variants

IIIA: Pre-production model.
IIIB: Combat capable two-seat trainer model of IIIA.
IIIBE: Two-seat trainer model of IIIE,
IIIC: Production model of IIIA.
IIID: Australian built two-seat model of IIIO.
IIIE: Long-range fighter/bomber.
IIIO: Australian built IIIE.
IIIR: Reconnaissance model of IIIE.
IIIRD: IIIR with improved Doppler navigation system.
IIIS: IIIE with a Hughes fire-control and Falcon AAMs.

French air force Mirage IIIC of EC2/10 armed with a Matra R.530 and a pair of AIM-9 Sidewinder AAMs.
(E.Moreau/Dassault via API)

Dassault Mirage 50 (France)

Type: Single-seat multi-mission fighter.

Development/History

The Mirage 50 is based on the Mirage III/5 series airframe, but is powered by the Atar 9K-50 turbojet from the Mirage F1. The Atar 9K-50 gives a substantial increase in thrust over the standard Mirage III/5. The performance is further enhanced including either the Agave or Cyrano IVM multi-function radar.

The prototype Mirage 50 first flew on 15 April 1979. Twenty years on, an extensive upgrade programme by the two Mirage 50 operators includes the fitting of canards as well as equipment and avionics upgrades. This has resulted in Dassault assigning the designation Mirage 50M to describe these modified aircraft.

Specification

Powerplant
1 x SNECMA Atar 9K-50 turbojet.
Power: 49.2 kN (11,055 lb st) dry, 70.6 kN (15,873 lb st) with afterburner.

Dimensions
Length: 15.65 m (51 ft 4 1/4 ins)
Span: 8.22m (26 ft 11 1/2 ins)
Height: 4.50 m (14 ft 9 ins)

Weights
Empty: 7,150 kg (15,765 lb)
Max T/O: 14.700 kg (32,400 lb)

Performance
Max Speed: 1,390 km/h (863 mph)
Range: 2,410 km (1,498 miles)

Armament
2 x 30 mm canon plus Magic or R.530 AAM depending on radar fit.

Status Production complete.

Customers
Chile (FC/CH upgraded to Pantera 50C), France, Venezuela (EV/DV).

Manufacturer
Dassault - France

Dassault Mirage 50M armed with Matra R.550 Magic AAMs shows off the canards and a wing extension just below the canards.
(AMD-BA/Aviaplans via API)

Dassault Mirage 50

Variants

50: Basic production model.
50M: Modification to incorporate canards and other equipment/avionics.
Pantera: Chilean name for 50M.

Dassault Mirage 50EV of the Venezuelan air force with a refuelling probe.
(Robineau/Dassault/ Aviaplans via API)

Dassault Mirage F1 (France)

Type: Single-seat multi-mission fighter and attack aircraft.

Development/History

Mirage F1 development began in 1964 following an order from the French Government for a Mirage III replacement. Several prototype designs were built including ones with variable geometry (Mirage G) and VTOL (IIIV). Designated Mirage F2, a two-seat prototype was first flown on 12 June 1966 followed by the private venture smaller single-seat on 23 December 1966.

The F1 prototype was lost the following May but had proved that this was the preferred model and a further three pre-production F1s were ordered. A 40 per cent increase in fuel capacity gives the F1 three times the endurance of the Mirage III, as well as a better handling at low level and higher speeds.

R Jordanian Mirage F1-EJ   *(Jeremy Flack)*

Specification of Mirage F1-C.

Powerplant
1 x SNECMA Atar 9K-50 turbojet.
Power: 49.2 kN (11,055 lb st) dry, 70.6 kN (15,873 lb st) with afterburner.

Dimensions
Length: 15.0 m (49 ft 2 1/2 ins)
Span: 8.40 m (27 ft 6 3/4 ins)
Height: 4.50 m (14 ft 9 ins)

Weights
Empty: 7,400 kg (16,314 lb)
Max T/O: 14,900 kg (32,850 lb)

Performance
Max Speed: Mach 2.2 at altitude.
Range: 1,400 km (870 miles) at low level.

Armament
2 x 30 mm cannon plus seven external stores positions for up to a total 4,000 kg (8,820 lb) load. Typically, this would carry a AIM-9 Sidewinder or 550 Magic AAM on each wing tip, a R.530 or Super 530 on the centreline and two inner positions. Alternatively, a range of ASMs, bombs, rocket and other pods can be carried.

Status
Production complete.

Customers
Ecuador (JA/JE), France (B/C/C-200/CR/CT), Greece (CG), Iraq (BQ/EQ), Jordan (CJ/EJ), Kuwait (BK/CK), Libya (AD/BD/ED), Morocco (CH/EH), Qatar (DDA/EDA), South Africa (AZ/CZ), Spain (CE.14A(BE)/C.14A(CE)/C.14B(EE)).

Manufacturer
Dassault - France
Atlas - South Africa

Dassault Mirage F1 (France)

Variants

F2: Larger two-seat prototype.
F1: Single-seat prototype
F1-A: Single-seat basic VFR multi-purpose model.
F1-B: Two-seat trainer
F1-C: Single-seat all-weather interceptor.
F1-D: Two-seat trainer of F1-E.
F1-E: Improved F1-A for export.
F1-R: Single-seat day and night reconnaissance model.
F1-CR: F1-R for French air force.
F1-CT: F1-C-200 modified with radar and avionic upgrades giving additional attack role.
F1-C-200: F1-C with refuelling probe.

Spanish air force Mirage
C.14A (F1-CE).
(Jeremy Flack)

Left: Close up of a radar guided Matra R.530 under a Mirage F1-C.
(Jeremy Flack)

Above: French air force Mirage F1-CR of ER1/33 armed with a pair of Matra R.550 Magic AAMs.
(Armee de l'Air via API)

Dassault Mirage 2000 (France)

Type: Single-seat interceptor and multi-role fighter.

Development/History

In 1975 the French Government announced that the Mirage 2000 had been selected to be the next generation fighter for the French air force, and the prototype was first flown on 10 March 1978. Careful design enables extra fuel to be carried internally by blending the wings roots into the fuselage, while the use of titanium and boron/carbon fibre panels has helped to reduce overall weight. The first production Mirage 2000 took to the air on 20 November 1982 and deliveries to the French air force commenced the following year.

French air force Mirage 2000C of EC5/330.

Specification for Mirage 2000C

Powerplant
1 x SNECMA M53-P2 turbofan
Power: 64.3 kN (14,462 lb st) dry, 95.1 kN (21,385 lb st) with afterburner.

Dimensions
Length: 14.36 m (47 ft 1 1/4 ins)
Span: 9.13 m (29 ft 11 1/2 ins)
Height: 5.20 m (17 ft 0 3/4 ins)

Weights
Empty: 7,500 kg (16,534 lb)
Max T/O: 17,000 kg (37,480 lb)

Performance
Max Speed: Mach 2.2
Range: 1,852 km (1,151 miles) hi-hi-hi

Armament
2 x 30 mm guns + nine attachments for up to a total of 6,300 kg (3,200 lb) of external stores. Typically this can comprise a pair of Super 530D/F and a pair of Magic air-to-air missiles.

Status
In production.

Customers
Abu Dhabi (DAD/EAD/RAD), Egypt (EM/BM), France (B/C/D/N/-5), Greece (EG/ BG), India (Varja 2000H/TH), Peru (P/DP), Qatar (-5EDA/-5DDA), Taiwan (-5Ei/-5Di)

Manufacturer
Dassault Aviation - France

(Jeremy Flack)

Single and two-seat combat capable trainer multi-role Mirage 2000-5.

(Robineau/Aviaplans via API)

Dassault Mirage 2000 (France)

Variants

2000B: Two seat trainer variant of 2000C

2000BOB: (Banc Optronique Biplace - two-seat Optronics Testbed) 2000B used for FLIR, NVG and various other optical trials

2000C: Standard interceptor with various sub variants (eg S3, S4)

2000RDM: 2000C and 2000B also referred to 2000DA

2000DA (Defense Aèrienne): Surviving 2000Cs offered to Pakistan but not purchased.

2000RDI: 2000C with upgraded radar and M53-P2 power plants

2000D: Two seat conventional attack variant of 2000N

2000E: Multi-role fighter for export

2000ED: Two-seat trainer variant of 2000E

2000N: Two-seat low-altitude penetration variant with nuclear weapon capability

2000N: Initial designation of 2000D

2000R: Single-seat day/night reconnaissance export variant of 2000E but fitted with normal radar nose.

2000-3: Private venture for upgrade to CRT screen cockpit similar to Rafale.

2000-4: Private venture to integrate Matra Mica air-to-air missile.

2000-5: Multi-role upgrade incorporating -3 & -4 plus other avionics and weapon carrying enhancements.

2000S: Export variant of 2000D

French air force Mirage 2000C-RDI armed with a pair of Matra R.550 Magic II and Mica AAMs over the desert during the Gulf War.
(SIRPA Air via API)

French air force Mirage 2000C-5 armed with a four of Matra Mica and a pair of Matra Magic 2 AAMs.

Dassault Rafale (France)

Type: Two-seat or single-seat interceptor, multi-role fighter and reconnaissance fighter.

Development/History

The Rafale was conceived to replace French air force Jaguars and French navy Crusader and Super Etendards. The prototype Rafale took to the air for the first time on 4 July 1986. Despite aggressive marketing to potential export customers, Dassault has so far only achieved orders for the French air force and navy. Successive reductions in French defence spending have resulted in the delivery dates being postponed.

Below and right: Pre-production Dassault Rafale B in markings of French air force and armed with Magic II AAMs.
(Robineau/Dassault/Aviaplans via API)

Specification for Rafale C

Powerplant
2 x SNECMA M88-2 augmented turbofans
Power: 48.7 kN (10,500 lb st) dry, 72.9 kN (10,950 lb st) with afterburner.

Dimensions
Length: 15.30 m (50 ft 2 1/2 ins)
Span: 10.90 m (35 ft 9 1/4 ins) inc. wing tip missiles
Height: 5.34 m (17 ft 6 1/4 ins

Weights
Empty: 9,060 kg (19,973 lb)
Max T/O: No available

Performance
Max Speed: Mach 2 (at altitude)
Range: 1,852 km (1,151 miles) armed + external fuel

Armament
1 x 30 mm cannon and a total of 14 external stores attachments giving total maximum load of 8,000 kg. Typically, these could comprise 8 Mica AAM plus 2 fuel tanks.

Status
In production

Customers
Ordered for French air force and French navy

Manufacturer
Dassault Aviation - France

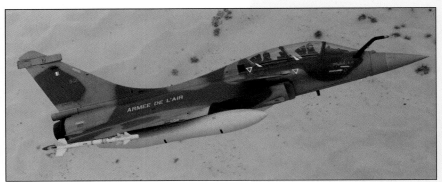

ARMEE DE L'AIR

Dassault Rafale (France)

Variants

Rafale B: Two-seat combat variant for French air force for pilot and Weapons Systems Operator or a single pilot capability.

Rafale C: Single-seat combat variant for the French air force

Rafale D: Original configuration from which production

variants derived. Since refers to 'Rafale Discret' (stealthy) - generic name for the French air force variants.

Rafale M: Single-seat carrier-borne fighter. Has 80 per cent commonalty of structure and systems with Rafale C and 95 per cent for avionics.

A Magic II AAM being launched at a target that is well off the boresight.
(Matra BAe Dynamics via API)

Pre-production Dassault Rafale M in the process of a catapult launch from the new carrier Charles de Gaulle.

(Robineau/Dassault/Aviaplans via API)

ADA Light Combat Aircraft (LCA) (India)

Type: All-weather multi-role fighter

Development/History

The LCA development programme for a MiG-21 replacement was approved by the Indian Government in 1983. The project definition was not completed until 1988 and the basic design finalised in 1990. Construction of the prototype commenced in 1991 and the first aircraft was rolled out in November 1995. The General Electric F404 is powering the first two prototypes, but this will be replaced by the Indian-built 83.4 kN (18,740 lb) GTRE Kaveri turbofan in subsequent prototypes and the production LCA. It is anticipated that the Indian air force and navy will have a combined requirement for up to 200 aircraft.

Variants

Single-seat model.
Two-seat trainer.
MCA: Study for advanced LCA model as Medium Combat Aircraft.

Specification

Powerplant
1 x General Electric F404-GE-F2J3 afterburning turbofan
Power: 80.5 kN (18,100 lb st) dry,

Dimensions
Length: 13.20 m (43 ft 3 3/4 ins)
Span: 8.20 m (26 ft 10 3/4 ins)
Height: 4.40 m (14 ft 5 1/4 ins)

Weights
Empty: 5,500 kg (12,125 lb) (approx)
Max T/O: 12,500 kg (27,558 lb) (approx)

Performance
Max Speed: Mach 1.8 (at altitude)
Range: Not available.

Armament
1 x 23 mm twin barrel gun plus 7 external stores stations with a capability of over 4,000 kg (8,818 lb). To these can be fitted a range of air-to-air missiles, rockets, bombs, drop tanks and pods.

Status
In development.

Customers
None

Manufacturer
Hindustan Aeronautics Ltd (HAL) - India - to a design by the Aeronautical Development Agency (ADA)

Right: The first LCA was rolled out in 1995.

Eurofighter 2000 (International)

Type: Single-seat fighter with secondary ground attack capability

Development/History

Plans for the Eurofighter commenced with the issuing of an outline staff target for a common fighter in December 1983 by the air chiefs of staff from France, Germany, Italy, Spain and the UK. An initial feasibility study commenced in July 1984 but by the following July the French had withdrawn. The work share arrangements were redrawn according to their proposed aircraft requirement giving Germany and the UK 33 per cent each, Italy 21 per cent and Spain 13 per cent. By the end of 1988 contracts for the weapon systems and engines had been placed.

In 1992 a thorough reappraisal of the EFA project was demanded by Germany to reduce overall cost of the project.

Specification

Powerplant
2 x Eurojet EJ200 advanced technology turbofans
Power: 60 kN (13,490 lb st) dry, 90 kN (20,250 lb st) with afterburner.

Dimensions
Length: 15.96 m (52 ft 4 1/4 ins)
Span: 10.95 m (35 ft 11 ins) over ECM pods
Height: 5.28 m (17 ft 3 7/8 ins)

Weights
Empty: 9,750 kg (21,495 lb)
Max T/O: 21,000 kg (46,297 lb)

Performance
Max Speed: Mach 2.0
Range: Not available

Armament
1 x 27 mm gun plus 13 external stores stations with a capacity of up to 6,500 kg (14,3330 lb) of fuel and/or missiles such as AIM-120 AMRAAM, Aspide and short range air-to-air missiles plus various air to surface weapons.

Status
In production

Customers
Requirements for Germany (180), Italy (121), Spain (87) and UK (232)

Manufacturer
DASA - Germany, Alenia - Italy, CASA - Spain, BAe - UK - managed by Eurofighter - Germany

Left and above: The first Eurofighter 2000 prototype armed with a pair of AIM-9 Sidewinder and four AIM-120 AMRAAM AAMs.

(BAe via API)

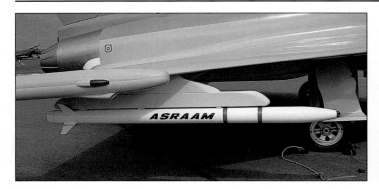

Delays plagued the programme due to political and economic grounds as well as a revision of perceived requirements on behalf of the Germans. This was resolved with an adjustment to the work sharing to Germany 30 per cent, the UK 37.5, Italy 19.5 and Italy 13 per cent respectively.

No prototype for the EFA has been built. The BAe EAP was built as a technology demonstrator and seven development aircraft have been completed. The latter were fitted with RB199 turbofans. Some of these are being replaced by the EJ200 which will be fitted to production aircraft. Staged improvements to the engine will increase power to 117 kN (26,300 lb)

ASRAAM AAM mock-up on Eurofighter.
(Jeremy Flack)

Variants
Single-seat: Standard fighter variant
Two-seat: Combat capable conversion trainer

Eurofighter 2000 cockpit.
(Jeremy Flack)

Eurofighter 2000 armed with AIM-9 Sidewinder and AIM-120 AMRAAM AAMs.

(Jeremy Flack)

Panavia Tornado ADV (International)

Type: Two-seat air defence interceptor, air superiority fighter and combat patrol aircraft.

Development/History

The origins of the Tornado can be traced back to the late 1960s when six NATO governments decided to investigate collaboration on a new combat aircraft. Canada and Belgium dropped out, but proposals for the then-named MRCA (Multi-Role Combat Aircraft) progressed. In 1969 the Netherlands also dropped out, leaving Germany, Italy and the UK to proceed with an even split of the workload. The first of 9 prototypes took to the air on 14 August 1974. Six pre-production examples followed. The first ADV development

RAF Tornado F. Mk3 of the F.3 OCU.

(Jeremy Flack)

Specification Tornado F. Mk3

Powerplant
2 x Turbo Union RB199-34R Mk.104 turbofans
Power: 40.5 kN (9,100 lb st) dry, 73.5 kN (16,520 lb st) with afterburner - Uninstalled rating.

Dimensions
Length: 18.68 m (61 ft 3 1/2 ins)
Span: 13.91 m (45 ft 7 1/2 ins) spread
8.60 m (28 ft 2 1/2 ins) swept
Height: 5.95 m (19 ft 6 1/4 ins)

Weights
Empty: 14,500 kg (31,970 lb) - operational
Max T/O: 27,986 kg (61,700 lb)

Performance
Max Speed: Mach 2.2
Range: 3,704 km (2,302 miles)

Armament
1 x 27 mm gun plus eight external attachment points permitting a total of 8,500 kg (18,740 lb) weapons and fuel. Normal load is 4 Skyflash missiles under fuselage, semi-recessed, plus a pair of Sidewinders mounted on either side of the drop tank pylons.

Status Production complete

Customers
Germany (IDS/ECR), Italy (IDS/F.3), Saudi Arabia (IDS/ADV), UK (GR.1/GR.1A/GR.1B/F.3/GR.4)

Manufacturer
DASA (previously MBB) - Germany
Alenia (previously Fiat then Aeritalia) - Italy
BAe (previously BAC) - UK

RAF Tornado F. Mk3 of No 65(R) Sqn armed with a pair of AIM-9 Sidewinder and SkyFlash AAMs.

(BAe via API)

Panavia Tornado ADV (International)

example was not ordered until 1976 but confidence in the IDS led to the first production order being placed shortly after. The ADV was urgently required by the RAF to replace its Lightnings and Phantoms. The first of three ADV prototypes took to the air on 27 October 1979.

The first 18 Tornados built were fitted with RB199 Mk.103 engines and designated F.2. The first flew initially on 12 April 1984 and deliveries were completed by the end of 1985. The first F.3 took to the air on 20 November 1985 and deliveries followed the next year. The F.3 is substantially superior over

the F.2 and as soon as sufficient F.3 deliveries were made the F.2s were placed in storage. Following a contractor's poor work practice a number of F.3 wings were severely damaged and those from the F.2 used to replace them.

An Italian shortfall in fighter capability resulted in 24 Tornado F.3s being leased from the RAF, pending arrival of the Eurofighter. The first F.3 arrived in Italy in 1995 after being modified to be Aspide AAM compatible. They also received the full Gulf War fit of avionic updates and defence aids including chaff and flares.

RAF Tornado F. Mk3 leased to the Italian air force. (Jeremy Flack)

Formation of Tornado F. Mk 3s from the F3 OCU and No 25 Sqn. (Jeremy Flack)

Panavia Tornado ADV (International)

Variants

ADV: Fighter variant
ECR: Electronic combat and electronic reconnaissance variant of IDS.
IDS: Standard ground attack variant
GR.1: UK IDS variant
GR.1: UK reconnaissance variant with SLIR & Linescan systems
GR.1B: UK maritime attack variant modified from GR.1s
F.2: Interim UK ADV variant
F.2A: Proposed modification of F.2s avionics to F.3 standard – not proceeded with. The DERA modified F.2 now unofficially designated F.2A
F.3: Definitive UK ADV variant
GR.4: Mid-Life Update (MLU) of GR.1
GR.4A: MLU of GR.1A
2000: Proposed successor for GR.4 with revised length and shape of nose.

Top left: Loading a SkyFlash AAM onto a Tornado F.3 prior to a peacekeeping mission over Bosnia.
(Jeremy Flack)

Above: Launching a SkyFlash AAM from an RAF Tornado F.3 of No 229 OCU.
(BAe via API)

Below: RAF Tornado F.3 of No 5 Sqn armed with a pair of AIM-9 Sidewinder plus four SkyFlash AAMs.
(Jeremy Flack)

RAF Tornado F.3 of No 5 Sqn armed with a pair of AIM-9 Sidewinder plus four SkyFlash AAMs escorts a Tu-95 'Bear' of the Russian air force. During the Cold War there were frequent encounters during probing flights. Nowadays they are few and far between. *(Jeremy Flack)*

IAI Kfir (Israel)

Type: Single-seat strike, ground attack and fighter.

Development/History

The Kfir came into being following the embargoing of an order for 50 Mirage 5Js by the French Government following the Six-Day War in June 1967. The Israeli proposal was to build a modified Mirage III/5 but power it with the General Electric J79 turbojet. This proved to be more difficult than planned and an interim model retaining the original Atar was built as a stopgap and named the Nesher.

The Kfir was first flown in June 1973 but not revealed until April 1975. Although similar to the Mirage, the Kfir is easily recognisable by the rear fuselage which is shorter and fatter. In April 1985 12 early production Kfir-C1s were leased to the USN/USMC for three years to be flown as aggressors. They were designated F-21A.

Specification for Kfir-C7

Powerplant
1 x General Electric J-79-J1E turbojet
Power: 52.89 kN (11,890 lb st) dry, 83.41 kN (18,750 lb st) with afterburner.

Dimensions
Length: 15.65 m (51 ft 4 1/4 ins) including probe
Span: 8.22 m (26 ft 11 1/2 ins)
Height: 4.55 m (14 ft 11 1/4 ins)

Weights
Empty: 7,285 kg (16.060 lb) estimated
Max T/O: 16,500 kg (36,376 lb)

Performance
Max Speed: Mach 2.3 at altitude
Range: 3,232 km (2,008 miles) ferry with 3,000 litres external fuel.

Armament
2 x 30 mm cannon plus nine external attachment points for up to 5,775 kg (12,730 lb) stores. Typical load is four Sidewinder, Python 3 or Shafrir 2 AAMs under the wings and a centreline drop tank. Alternatively, a range of AGMs, bombs, rocket pods, drop tanks or other podded systems.

Status Production complete.

Operators
Colombia (-C7/-TC7), Ecuador (-C2/-TC2), Israel (-C1/-C2/-TC2/-C7/-TC7), USA (F-21A)

Manufacturer
IAI (Israel Aircraft Industry) - Israel

The IAI Kfir-C2 demonstrator.   (Jeremy Flack)

*Israeli DF
IAI Kfir-C7
armed with
Shafrir 2
AAMs.*
(IAI via API)

IAI Kfir (Israel)

Variants

Kfir-C1: Initial production model.

Kfir-C2: Development of –C1, fitted with canards on air intakes and modification to wings and additions of nose strakes.

Kfir-TC2: Two-seat trainer model.

Kfir-C7: Improved –C2 with improved augmented thrust and weapon points as well as avionics and other cockpit improvements.

Kfir-TC7: Two-seat model of –C7.

F–21A: C1s incapable of converting to –C2 standard fitted with smaller canards.

Right: Cockpit of Kfir-C7.
(IAI via API)

Far right: Formation of Israeli DF Kfir-C7s armed with two or four Shafrir 2 AAMs.
(IAI via API)

50

IAI Lavi (Israel)

Type: Single-seat close air support and interdiction aircraft with secondary capability for air defence.

Development/History

Like the US Hornet, the Lavi (Young Lion) was designed for the attack role but was also to be capable of defending itself against enemy fighters. Looking similar to a two-seat F-16, it is slightly smaller and composite materials make up approximately 22 per cent of the structural weight.

The development programme was given the go-ahead in 1980 and prototype construction commenced in 1982. The first flight took place on 31 December 1986. Intended to replace Kfirs and Skyhawks of the Israeli Defence Force, a requirement for some 300 aircraft was envisaged. However, financial and political difficulties took their toll and on 30 August 1987 the project was cancelled following a 12-11 government vote with one abstention.

Controversy continued when a US intelligence satellite detected what was thought to be a prototype Lavi outside the Chengdu facility in China. This aircraft closely resembled the Lavi, but the connection was strongly refuted by the Israelis. However, a subsequently released photo of a wind tunnel model confirmed the very close resemblance. Various countries have shown keen interest in participating in the CAC J-10 project including the Russia and Israel.

Variants

Single-seat multi-role aircraft
Two-seat combat capable aircraft

Specification

Powerplant
1 x Pratt & Whitney PW1120 turbojet
Power: 91.7 kN (20,629 lb st)

Dimensions
Length: 14.57 m (47 ft 9 2/3 ins)
Span: 8.78 m (28 ft 9 2/3 ins)
Height: 4.78 m (15 ft 8 1/4 ins)

Weights
Empty:
Max T/O: 19,277 kg (42,500 lb)

Performance
Max Speed: Mach 1.8 at altitude
Range: Not available

Armament
1 x 30 mm cannon plus eleven external attachment points with wing tip mounted AAMs. A range of AGMs, bombs, rocket pods and other stores together with drop tanks on inner positions could be carried.

Status
Development programme cancelled.

Operators
None

Manufacturer
IAI (Israeli Aircraft Industries) - Israel

The prototype two-seat IAI Lavi with a Kfir-C7 chase plane.
(IAI via API)

Mitsubishi F-2 (Japan)

Type: Single-seat support fighter

Development/History

A modified version of the F-16C was selected as the
replacement for the Mitsubishi F-1 in October 1987. Initially
designated FS-X, a pair of single-seat and a pair of two-seat
prototypes were ordered together with two static test
airframes and construction commenced in 1994. The first
aircraft took to the air on 7 October 1995. The first
prototype, designated XF-2A, was handed over to the
Japanese Defence Agency (JDA) for development trials. The
JASDF has a requirement for 72 F-2A and 50 F-2Bs for the
training role. Current plans are to order 130 F.2A/F-2Bs for
initial delivery in 1999/2000.

Specification

Powerplant

1 x General Electric F110-GE-129 turbofan
Power: 131.7 kN (29,600 lb st) with afterburner

Dimensions

Length: 15.52 m (50 ft 11 ins)
Span: 11.13 m (36 ft 6 1/4 ins) over missile rails
Height: 4.96 m (16 ft 3 1/4 ins)

Weights

Empty: 12,000 kg (26,455 lb) equipped
Max T/O: 22,100 kg (48,722 lb)

Performance

Max Speed: Mach 2 at altitude.
Range: Not available.

Armament

1 x 20 mm multi-barrel gun plus up to 13
external stores stations available. Typical load
includes AIM-7F/M Sparrow and AIM-9
Sidewinder or AAM-3 AAMs plus drop tanks on
centreline and two inner stations. Other stores
include ASM-1/2 anti shipping missiles plus
various bombs and rocket pods.

Status

In development

Customers

Orders expected for at least 130 for JASDF

Manufacturer

Mitsubishi Heavy Industries - Japan

54

Variants
XF-2A: Prototype
F-2A: Single-seat variant
F-2B: Two-seat trainer variant

Mikoyan-Gurevich MiG-21 'Fishbed' (Russia)

Type: Single-seat multi-role fighter

Development/History

The MiG-21 was designed as an air superiority fighter using the experience gained by Soviet pilots during the Korean war. First flown on 16 June 1955 as the E-5, it was first publicly displayed at the Soviet Aviation Day at Tushino on the 24 June. The first production model was the MiG-21F and was short in range, avionics and weapons. Produced in limited numbers it was soon superseded by progressively improving production models. In addition, specially built one-offs in the E-33 and E-66 series were quickly establishing a number of world record flights.

The MiG-21 soon established itself as a major player and became the main fighter for all the Warsaw Pact air forces and was also exported to numerous countries throughout the world. Although Soviet production had long finished, MiG-21 production continued until 1986-7 in India.

An early Soviet air force MiG-21PF 'Fishbed-D'. *(Jeremy Flack)*

Specification MiG-21MF

Powerplant
1 x Tumansky RD-13-300 turbojet
Power: 5,100 kg (11,240 lb st) dry, 6,600 lb (14,500 lb st) with afterburner.

Dimensions
Length: 15.76 m (51 ft 8 1/2 ins) including probe
Span: 7.15 m (23 ft 5 1/2 ins)
Height: 4.50 m (14 ft 9 ins)

Weights
Empty: 5,843 kg (12,882 lb)
Max T/O: 9,800 kg (21,605 lb)

Performance
Max Speed: Mach 2.1 at altitude.
Range: 1,800 km (1,118 miles) ferry with three drop tanks.

Armament
1 x 23 mm gun plus four external attachment points. Typically, two K-13A (AA-2 'Atoll') on out pylons and two K-13A (AA-2-2 'Advanced Atoll') AAMs on inner pylons. Alternatively, a range of rocket pods, bombs or drop tanks can be carried.

Status
Production complete.

Operators
Afghanistan (F/U), Algeria (F/MF/bis/U), Angola (MF/U/UM), Bangladesh (MF/U), Bulgaria (PFM/RF/U), Cuba (F/PFM/PFMA/bis/U), Congo, Czechoslovakia (PF/MF/RF/U), East Germany (F/PFM/MF/US/UM), Ethiopia (PF/U), Egypt (F/FL/PFS/PFM/MF/R/U/US), Finland (F/bis/US/UM), Guinea (PFM), Hungary (MF/bis/UM), India (FL/bis/M/MF/PFMA/U/UM), Indonesia (F), Iraq (MF/bis/U), Laos (F/PF/U), Madagascar (FL), Mali, Mozambique (MF), Nigeria (MF/U), North Korea (F/PF/PFM/U), Poland (MF/bis/RF/U), Romania (F/PF/MF/U), Somalia (MF/U), Sudan (PFM), Syria (PF/PFM/bis/U), Uganda, Russia, Upper Volta, Vietnam, Yemen (F/U), Yugoslavia (F/PFMS/bis/U/US) Zambia (MF/U).

Manufacturer
Mikoyan-Gurevich - Russia
HAL (Hindustan Aeronautics Ltd - India
CAC (Chengdu Aircraft Corporation) - China

Czech air force MiG-21UM 'Mongol' with a paint-scheme compatible with the age of the aircraft.

(Jeremy Flack)

Mikoyan-Gurevich MiG-21 'Fishbed' (Russia)

Variants

E-5: Prototype.

MiG-21 'Fishbed-A': Initial limited production model.

MiG-21F 'Fishbed-C': Improved production model.

MiG-21P 'Fishbed-D': All round improvements giving all-weather capability. Fuselage similar to MiG-21F with enlarged intake and centrebody plus pitot tube moved to top of intake.

MiG-21FL 'Fishbed-E': Export model without blown flap or RATOG capability.

MiG-21PFS, or MiG-21PF(SPS): Similar to MiG-21PF with blown flaps.

MiG-21PFM 'Fishbed-F': Further improved export model of 'PFS with 45 cm (18 in) longer vertical tail and small dorsal fillet removed.

Analogue: Single research model with Tu-144 wing and no tail.

MiG-21PFMA 'Fishbed-J': Similar to 'PFM with two extra wing pylons and deeper dorsal fairing. Pitot tube also off-set.

MiG-21M 'Fishbed-J': Similar to 'PFMA with internal gun.

MiG-21R 'Fishbed-H': Tactical reconnaissance model. Belly gun replaced by camera pack just aft of nosewheel bay. Also has external centreline pod with additional cameras and sensors.

MiG-21MF 'Fishbed-J': Similar to PFMA with Tumansky R-13-300. Lighter airframe giving improved performance. Has debris deflector beneath each suction relief door.

MiG-21RF 'Fishbed-H': Reconnaissance model of 'MF with 'R kit.

MiG-21SMT 'Fishbed-K': Similar to 'MF with ECM wingtip

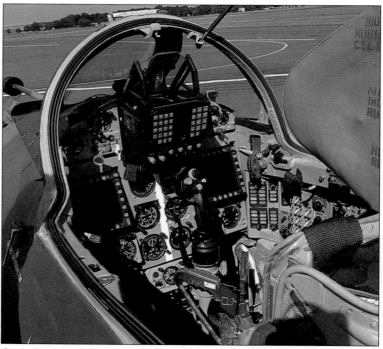

Cockpit of the refurbished MiG-21MF undertaken jointly by Aerostar and Elbit.

(Jeremy Flack)

pods and deep dorsal spine extending to brake chute housing.

MiG-21bis 'Fishbed-L': Generally improved model with Tumansky R-25 engine together with updated avionics. Larger dorsal fairing for increased fuel capacity.

MiG-21bis 'Fishbed-N': Advanced version of 'Fishbed-L' with further improved avionics. Has ILS antennae under nose and on tail.

MiG-21U 'Mongol': Two-seat trainer model of MiG-21F.

MiG-21US 'Mongol': Blown flap added.

MiG-21UM 'Mongol': Two-seat trainer model of 'MF plus four stores points.

E-33 'Mongol': Model(s) used to establish women's records.

E-66 'Fishbed-C': Re-engined model to set speed record.

E-66A 'Fishbed-C': E-66 variant used to set height record.

E-76 'Fishbed-D': Model(s) used to establish womens' records.

Indian air force MiG-21bis
(HAL via API)

The Aerostar/Elbit MiG-21MF Lancer is one of a number of upgrade programmes. With an estimated 12,000 examples delivered to 56 air forces there is substantial business in the modernisation business.
(Jeremy Flack)

Mikoyan MiG-23/27 'Flogger' (Russia)

Type: Single-seat variable-geometry air combat fighter and two-seat operational trainer.

Development/History

The prototype MiG-23 was designed to be the replacement for the MiG-21. It was designated Ye-231G and displayed at the Domodedovo Airport for the first time in July 1967, shortly after its first flight. Pre-production MiG-23s were delivered to the Soviet air force in 1970 and series production followed in 1973. When Mikoyan ended MiG-23 production in the mid 1980s some 1,800 examples had been built. However, production continued in India.

Numerous upgrade programmes are being proposed to enhance existing aircraft. One trial evaluation saw the French Magic 2 AAM on a Czech air force MiG-23ML.

(Matra via API)

Specification of MiG-23ML 'Flogger-G'

Powerplant
1 x Tumansky R-35-300 turbojet
Power: 127.5 kN (28,660 lb st) with afterburner.

Dimensions
Length: 16.71 m (54 ft 10 ins) including probe
Span: 13.965 m (45 ft 10 ins) fully spread
7.779 m (25 ft 6 1/2 ins) fully swept
Height: 4.82 m (15 ft 9 3/4 ins)

Weights
Empty: 10,200 lb (22.485 lb)
Max T/O: 17,800 kg (39,250 lb)

Performance
Max Speed: Mach 2.35 at altitude.
Range: 1,950 km (1.212 miles)

Armament
1 x 23 mm twin barrelled gun plus seven external attachment points. Typical load is one R-23 ('Apex') AAM under each wing plus four R-60 ('Aphid') and a drop tank. Alternatively, various bombs, rocket pods can be fitted.

Status
Production complete

Customers
Afghanistan, Algeria (Flogger-E/F), Angola (C/E), Bulgaria (B/C/H), Cuba (C/E/F), Czechoslovakia (B/C/G/H), East Germany (B/C/G), Egypt (C/F), Ethiopia (F), Hungary (B/C), India (B/C/H), Iraq (E/H), Libya (C/E/F), North Korea (E), Poland (B/C/H), Romania (B/C), Russia (A/B/C/G/H/K)), Sudan, Syria (F/G), Vietnam (F), Yemen (F).

Manufacturer
Mikoyan - Russia
HAL - India

Czech air force MiG-23ML 'Flogger-G'.

(Jeremy Flack)

Mikoyan MiG-23/27 'Flogger' (Russia)

Variants

MiG-23 'Flogger-A': Ye-231G prototype.
MiG-23S 'Flogger-A': Pre-production model.
MiG-23SM 'Flogger-B': MiG-23S with four additional stores points.
MiG-23M 'Flogger-B': First series production model.
MiG-23MF 'Flogger-B': Improved, re-engined MiG-23M.
MiG-23UB 'Flogger-C': Two-seat training model of MiG-23S.
MiG-23UM 'Flogger-C': Two-seat combat capable operational trainer.
MiG-23MS 'Flogger-E': Export model of 'Flogger-B' with lower standard of radar and avionics.
MiG-23B 'Flogger-F': Single-seat export fighter/bomber with revised nose with laser rangefinder.
MiG-23BN 'Flogger-F': Similar to 'B with R29B-300 engine and Sokol-23N nav/attack system.
MiG-23ML 'Flogger-G': Lightened model similar to 'Flogger-

B' with R-35F-300 engine and smaller dorsal fin.
MiG-23P 'Flogger-G': Modified existing 'Flogger-G' with upgraded avionics capable of giving ground prompts to pilot to engage afterburner and launch missiles.
MiG-23BK 'Flogger-H': Similar to 'Flogger-F' with RWR fairing forward of nosewheel door.
MiG-23MLD 'Flogger-K': Modified 'Flogger-G' with dogtooth notch where the wing glove meets the fuselage. New IFF aerials located forward of canopy. R-73A (AA-11 'Archer') AAMs compatible and the outer wing pylons pivot.
MiG-27 'Flogger-D': Ground-attack model with laser range-finder in sharply tapered nose plus attack avionics and armour.
MiG-27M 'Flogger-J': Enhanced avionics in wider nose. Has an extension to wing root leading edge.
Bahadur 'Flogger-J': Indian name for their MiG-27M licence assembled/built variant.

Above and right:
Czech air force MiG-23ML
'Flogger-G'.

(Jeremy Flack)

Far right:
Cockpit of Czech air
force MiG-23ML.

(Jeremy Flack)

Mikoyan-Gurevich MiG-25 'Foxbat' (Russia)

Type: Single-seat interceptor, reconnaissance aircraft and two-seat conversion aircraft

Development/History

Design of the Ye-155P supersonic high-altitude interceptor started in 1959. The design was intended to deal with US nuclear bombers attacking at high speed/high altitudes, but eventually a look-down/shoot-down capability. The same basic design was also used to meet a requirement for a reconnaissance aircraft which was designated Ye-155R. The latter was the first to fly on 6 March 1964 followed by the Ye-155P on 9 September 1964.

Soviet air force MiG-25 'Foxbat'.

(Bob Archer)

Specification MiG-25PDS

Powerplant
2 x Soyuz/Tumansky R-15BD-300 turbojets
Power: 86.3 kN (19,400 lb st) dry, 109.75 kN (24,675 lb st) with afterburner.

Dimensions
Length: 23.82 m (78 ft 1 3/4 ins)
Span: 14.015 m (45 ft 11 3/4 ins)
Height: Height 6.10 m (20 ft 0 1/4 ins)

Weights
Empty: Not available.
Max T/O: 36,720 kg (80,950 lb)

Performance
Max Speed: Mach 2.83 at altitude.
Range: 1,250 km (777 miles).

Armament
Four external attachment points for R-40R (AA-6 'Acrid'), R-40T (AA-6 'Acrid'), R-60, R-23 (AA-7 'Apex'), R-73A (AA-11 'Archer') or R-60T (AA-8 'Aphid') AAMs.

Status
Production complete

Customers
Algeria (Foxbat-A/B/C), India (B/C), Iraq (A), Libya (A/E), Russia (A/B/C/D/E/F), Syria (A/B)

Manufacturer
Mikoyan & Gurevich - Russia

MiG-25 RBK

Mikoyan-Gurevich MiG-25 'Foxbat' (Russia)

Variants

Ye-155P: Interceptor prototype.

Ye-155R: Reconnaissance prototype.

Ye-155M 'Foxbat-E': Record breaking aircraft.

MiG-25 'Foxbat-A': Basic interceptor model.

MiG-25R 'Foxbat-B': Basic reconnaissance model.

MiG-25U 'Foxbat-C': Two-seat trainer model.

MiG-25R 'Foxbat-D': Reconnaissance model with larger SLAR.

MiG-25M 'Foxbat-E': Modified 'Foxbat-A' with limited shoot down capability.

MiG-25RB 'Foxbat-B': MiG-25R bomber capability added.

MiG-25RBV 'Foxbat-B': MiG-25RB with added SLAR capability.

MiG-25RBT 'Foxbat-B': MiG-25RB with added ELINT

capability.

MiG-25PU 'Foxbat-C': Two-seat trainer of MiG-25P.

MiG-25RU 'Foxbat-C': Two-seat trainer of MiG-25R.

MiG-25RBK 'Foxbat-D': Similar to RBV with Kub SLAR

MiG-25RBS 'Foxbat-D': Similar to RBK with Sabla SLAR

MiG-25RBSh 'Foxbat-D': Upgraded RBS with Shompol SLAR

MiG-25RBF 'Foxbat-D': Upgraded MiG-25RB with Shar ELINT

MiG-25PD 'Foxbat-E': Development of 'P with uprated R-15BD-300 engines.

MiG-25PDS 'Foxbat-E': Similar to 'PD but converted from 'P.

MiG-25BM 'Foxbat-F': Defence suppression derivative of MiG-25RB with ECM replacing reconnaissance module plus Kh-58 (AS-11) ARMs.

Soviet air force MiG-25 'Foxbat'.

(Bob Archer)

MiG-25P

MAPO MiG-29 'Fulcrum' (Russia)

Type: Single-seat all-weather counter-air fighter with attack capability, and two-seat combat trainer.

Development/History

An operational requirement was issued for a light fighter to replace the MiG-21, MiG-23, Su-15 and Su-17 in 1972. The prototype first flew on 6 October 1977. Following major design changes, the first production MiG-29s to the Frontal Aviation in 1983 and became operational two years later. The MiG-29 is designed for high manoeuvrability together with ability to successfully destroy targets from 200m to 60 km (660 ft to 37 miles).

Slovak air force MiG-29.

(Jeremy Flack)

Specification MiG-29 'Fulcrum-A'

Powerplant
2 x Klimov/Sarkisov RD-33 turbofans
Power: 49.4 kN (11,110 lb st) dry, 54.9-81.4 kN (12,345-18,300 lb st) with afterburner.

Dimensions
Length: 17.32 m (37 ft 3 1/4 ins) including probe
Span: 11.36 m (37 ft 3 1/4 ins)
Height: 4.73 m (15 ft 6 1/4 ins)

Weights
Empty: 10,900 kg (24,030 lb)
Max T/O: 18,500 kg (40,785 lb)

Performance
Max Speed: Mach 2.3 at height
Range: 1,500 km (932 miles) internal fuel only

Armament
1 x 30 mm gun plus seven external attachment points. Typically, six R-60T, R-60MK (AA-8) or R-73E (AA-11) close range AAMs or R-27R1 (AA-10A) medium range AAMs. Alternatively a range of bombs and rocket packs can be fitted.

Status In production.

Customers
Belarus, Bulgaria, Croatia, Cuba, Czech Republic, Germany, Hungary, India, Iran, Iraq, Kazakhstan, North Korea, Malaysia, Moldova, Poland, Romania, Russia, Slovakia, Syria, Turkmenistan, Ukraine, Uzbekistan, Yemen, Yugoslavia,

Manufacturer
MAPO (formerly Mikoyan) - Russia

Slovak air force MiG-29UB.

(Jeremy Flack)

MAPO MiG-29 'Fulcrum' (Russia)

Variants

MiG-29 'Fulcrum-A': Basic counter-air tactical fighter.
MiG-29UB 'Fulcrum-B': Two-seat combat trainer.
MiG-29 'Fulcrum-C': Curved top to fuselage for increased avionics and fuel capacity.
MiG-29S 'Fulcrum-C': Subject of multistage upgrade to improve avionics and missile carrying capability.
MiG-29SE 'Fulcrum-C': Export model of MiG-29S.
MiG-29SM: Upgraded MiG-29S with air to surface and anti ship missile capability.
MiG-29SD: 'Fulcrum-A' Export model of basic MiG-29 with most of 'SE upgrades.

MiG-29N: Local Malaysian designation for MiG-29SD
MiG-29NUB: Local Malaysian designation for MiG-29UB
MiG-29M: Advanced tactical fighter, ground support and naval precision weapon control.
MiG-29ME: Export model of MiG-29M - redesignated MiG-33
MiG-29K: Naval carrier based version with folding wings.
MiG-29KVP: Demonstrator for MiG-29K with STOL and arrester hook.
MiG-33: Export model of MiG-29M.
MiG-35: Further upgrade of MiG-33 with ten external attachment points, canards and thrust vectoring.

Above: Russian air force MiG-29A with undercarriage down.
(Jeremy Flack)

Right: Cockpit of Hungarian MiG-29A
(Jeremy Flack)

Above: Russian RW-AE/R-77 (AA-12) medium range AAM together with a Zvezda Kh-31 (AS-17 'Krypton') ARM on a MiG-29. (Jeremy Flack)

MAPO MiG-29 'Fulcrum' (Russia)

Slovak air force MiG-29A

(Jeremy Flack)

Mikoyan MiG-31 'Foxhound' (Russia)

Type: Two-seat strategic interceptor.

Development/History

The MiG-31 was designed as a long range interceptor to replace the Su-15 and MiG-23 in what was a key role for the PVO. Initially designated as the Ye-155MP and first flown on 16 September 1975, production commenced in 1979. The first regiments became operational in 1982. As with the MiG-25, from which the Ye-155MP was developed, a series of record-breaking flights were made. The Ye-155M was modified to Ye-266M and pushed the records still further. Typical was the 30,000 m (98,424 ft) time-to-height which was reduced to 3 min 9.85 seconds. Absolute height was raised to 37,650 m (123,624 ft).

Specification

Powerplant
2 x Aviadvigatel D-30F6 turbofans.
Power: 93.1 kN (20,950 lb) dry, 151.9 kN (34,170 lb) with afterburning.

Dimensions
Length: 22.69 m (74 ft 5 1/4 ins)
Span: 13.465 m (44 ft 2 ins)
Height: 6.15 m (20 ft 2 1/4 ins)

Weights
Empty: 21,840 kg (48,105 lb)
Max T/O: 46,200 kg (101,850 lb) with two drop tanks.

Performance
Max Speed: 3,000 km/h (1,865 mph) at altitude.
Range: 2,135 km (1,327 miles) supersonic cruise on internal fuel.

Armament
1 x 23 mm 6 barrel gun plus six external attachment points. Typically, four R-33 (AA-9 'Amos') under the fuselage plus two R-40T (AA-6 'Acrid') AAMs on the inner pylons or four R-60 (AA-8 'Aphid').

Status In production.

Customers
Russia, China.

Manufacturer
Mikoyan - Russia
Sokol - Russia

Russian air force MiG-31 'Foxhound'.
(Jeremy Flack)

73

Mikoyan MiG-31 'Foxhound' (Russia)

Russian air force MiG-31 'Foxhound'.

(Jeremy Flack)

Variants

Ye-155MP: Prototype.
Ye-266M: Modified Ye-155M for record breaking flights.
MiG-31 'Foxhound-A': Initial production.
MiG-31M 'Foxhound-B': Improved version with upgraded engine and plus all systems. Two extra external attachment points added.
MiG-31B: Upgrade to be compatible with R-37 AAM and refuelling probe.
MiG-31BS: Converted 'Foxhound-As' to be compatible with R-37 and RVV-AE (AA-12 'Adder') AAMs and refuelling probe.
MiG-31D: Dedicated anti-satellite model

Right: The MiG-31 has recessed positions under the fuselage to house four R-33 (AA-9 'Amos') missiles.

(Jeremy Flack)

Below: R-40 (AA-6 'Acrid') AAM.

(Jeremy Flack)

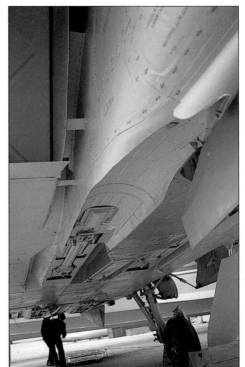

Mikoyan MiG-31 'Foxhound' (Russia)

R-33 (AA-9 'Amos') AAM.

(Jeremy Flack)

R-60 (AA-8 'Aphid') AAMs.

(Jeremy Flack)

Russian air force MiG-31 'Foxhound'.

(Jeremy Flack)

Mikoyan 1-42 (Russia)

Type: Single-seat multi-role tactical aircraft

Development/History

The Mikoyan 1-42 MFI (mnogofunktsionalnyy frontovoy-istrebityel or multi-role tactical aircraft) was selected in 1986 to be Russia's next generation fighter. Manufacture of two prototypes is believed to have been completed, although the specified engines were unavailable. Lyulka engines were fitted to enable high speed taxi trials to be conducted but it is believed that the first flight has been delayed due to funding difficulties.

Variants

None

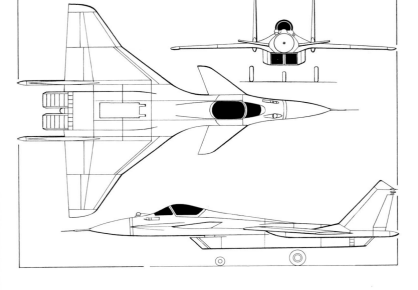

Specification

Powerplant

2 x Saturn/Lyulka AL-41F turbofans with afterburner and thrust vectoring nozzles.
Power: 180.2 kN (40,500lb st)

No other details known

Status

In development

Customers

None

Manufacturer

MAPO - Russia

Sukhoi Su-27 'Flanker' (Russia)

Type: Single-seat all-weather air-superiority fighter and single/two-seat ground attack aircraft, two-seat combat trainer

Development/History

Development of the Su-27 commenced in 1969 and it first took to the air on 20 May 1977 with the Sukhoi designation of T-10. Development problems led to a major airframe redesign and the revised T-10S first flew on 20 April 1981. Series production commenced the following year and entered service in 1985 as the Su-27.

The Su-27 appears very similar to the MiG-29, but is about a third larger, looks rather sleeker and has a large faring extending rearwards between the engines.

Specification for Su-27P

Powerplant
2 x Saturn/Lyulka AL-31F turbofans
Power: 122.6 kN (27,557 lb st) with afterburning.

Dimensions
Length: 21.94 m (71 ft 11 1/2 ins) excluding probe
Span: 14.70 m (48 ft 2 3/4 ins)
Height: 5.93 m (19 ft 5 1/2 ins)

Weights
Empty: 17,500 kg (38,580 lb)
Max T/O: 33,000 kg (72,750 lb)

Performance
Max Speed: Mach 2.35 at sea level
Range: 3,680 km (2,285 miles)

Armament
1 x 30 mm gun plus 11 external attachment points. Typically, up to ten air-to-air missiles including R-27R (AA-10 'Alamo-A'), R-27T (AA-10B 'Alamo-B'), R-27ER (AA-10C 'Alamo-C'), R-27ET (AA-10D 'Alamo-D'), R-73A (AA-11 'Archer'), R-60 (AA-8 'Aphid'), R-33 (AA-9 'Amos').

Status
In production.

Customers
Armenia, Azerbaijan, Belarus, China, Georgia, Kazakhstan, Russia, Ukraine, USA, Vietnam.

Manufacturer
Sukhoi - Russia

Sukhoi Su-27 'Flanker' (Russia)

Variants

T-10: Prototype (Sukhoi designation).
T-10S: Production prototype (Sukhoi designation).
T-10U: Two-seat trainer (Sukhoi designation). See Su-27UB
P-42: Stripped and lightened Su-27 model used for record breaking flights.
Su-27 'Flanker-A': Military designation for T-10.
Su-27P 'Flanker-B': Single-seat production air-defence variant with squared wings and extended tail cone.

Su-27S 'Flanker-B': Dual-role air combat/ground attack with ECM pods on wing tips.
Su-27SK 'Flanker-B': Export variant of Su-27S.
Su-27SMK: Single-seat multi-role fighter with 12 hard points.
Su-27PD: Basic Su-27P specially prepared for demonstration flying fitted with refuelling probe.
Su-27UB 'Flanker-C': Two-seat combat capable trainer. Military designation for T-10U.
Su-27UBK 'Flanker-C': Export model of Su-27UB.

Su-27M: Advanced development (see Su-35).Su-27LL-PS Su-27UB modified for thrust-vectoring development.

Su-27LMK: Similar to Su-27LL-PS.

Su-27K: Prototype of navalised Su-33.

Su-27IB: Two-seat (side by side) fighter bomber prototype of Su-32FN/Su-34.

Su-27PU: Prototype of Su-30.

Su-30: Two-seat long-range combat aircraft and trainer developed from Su-27UB.

Su-30M: Two-seat multi-role fighter developed from Su-27UB

Su-27MK: Export variant of Su-30M.

Su-32FN: Two-seat in tandem long-range shore-based maritime strike aircraft.

Su-33: Single-seat carrier-based air defence fighter with anti-ship capability. Fitted with folding wings.

Su-34: Similar to Su-32FN but role of long range theatre bomber.

J-11: Chinese licence built model.

Sukhoi Su-33 'Flanker-D' (Russia)

Type: Single-seat ship-based defence fighter with anti-ship capability.

Development/History

Development of the Su-33 began in 1976. Based on the Su-27, it has folding wings, a tail hook, and is immediately distinguishable by its foreplanes. The prototype flew for the first time on 17 August 1987 as the T-10K/Su-27K. Following carrier trials in 1989, production aircraft came off the production line the following year and by 1992 they achieved an initial operational capability. An initial batch of 20 Su-33s were ordered and have been seen operating on the Russian navy carrier *Kuznetsov*, but further orders are uncertain.

Variants

T-10K: Prototype (Sukhoi designation)
Su-27K: Prototype (Military designation)
Su-33: Production model.

Specification

Powerplant

2 x Saturn/Lyulka AL-31F turbofans
Power: 122.6 kN (27,557 lb st) with afterburner.

Dimensions

Length: 21.185 m (69 ft 6 ins) inc. nose probe
Span: 14.70 m (48 ft 2 3/4 ins)
Height: 5.90 m (19 ft 4 1/4 ins)

Weights

Empty: Not available
Max T/O: 30,500 kg (66,130 lb)

Performance

Max Speed: Mach 2.165 (VNE at 11,000m (36,000 ft)
Range: 3,000 km (1,865 miles) internal fuel only

Armament

1 x 30 mm gun plus 11 external attachment points. Typically, up to ten air-to-air missiles including R-27R (AA-10 'Alamo-A'), R-27T (AA-10B 'Alamo-B'), R-27ER (AA-10C 'Alamo-C'), R-27ET (AA-10D 'Alamo-D'), R-73A (AA-11 'Archer'), R-60 (AA-8 'Aphid'), R-33 (AA-9 'Amos').

Status

Production complete.

Customers

Russia

Manufacturer

Sukhoi - Russia

Russian navy Su-33 with wings and tail folded.

(Linda Jackson)

Sukhoi Su-35 (Russia)

Type: Single-seat all-weather counter air fighter and ground attack aircraft.

Development/History

A further development of the Su-27 design, the Su-35 first flew in prototype form in May 1985. Initially designated T-10S, then Su-27M and finally Su-35, it is an extensive modification of the basic Su-27 with canards and wing extensions. A total of 11 prototype and pre-series aircraft had been built of which the last was further modified for thrust-vectoring trials. Designated Su-37, it astounded SBAC Farnborough visitors with the *kilbit* manoeuvre, in which the aircraft performed a somersault at low level.

Sukhoi Su-35 touches down with large air brake deployed.   *(Jeremy Flack)*

Specification

Powerplant
2 x Saturn/Lyulka AL-35F (AL-35FM) turbofans.
Power: 137.3 kN (30,865 lb st)with afterburner.

Dimensions
Length: 22.20 m (72 ft 10 ins)
Span: 15.16 m (49 ft 8 3/4 ins) inc. ECM pods
Height: 6.36 m (20 ft 10 1/4 ins)

Weights
Empty: 17,000 kg (37,479 lb)
Max T/O: 34,000 kg (74,957 lb)

Performance
Max Speed: Mach 2.35 (at height)
Range: 4,000 km (2,485 miles) max internal fuel

Armament
1 x 30 mm cannon plus 14 external stores points for up to 8,000 kg (17,635 lb). These can include R-27 (AA-10 'Alamo'), R-40 (AA-6 'Acrid'), R-60 (AA-8 'Aphid'), R-73E (A-11 'Archer'), RVV-AE R77 (AA-12 'Adder') AAMs plus a range of ASMs, LGB, bombs and rocket pods.

Status
Thought to be in production.

Customers
Russia

Manufacturer
Sukhoi - Russia

Sukhoi Su-35 approached the runway with large air brake deployed.

(Jeremy Flack)

Sukhoi Su-35 (Russia)

Variants

T-10S: Prototype (Sukhoi designation)

Su-27M: Initial prototype designation (military designation)

Su-35: Basic production model.

Su-37: Thrust vectoring nozzle model of Su-35.

Sukhoi Su-35 lifts off with an impressive range of weaponry under its wings.

(Jeremy Flack)

Atlas Cheetah (South Africa)

Type: Single-seat fighter and reconnaissance aircraft and two-seat operational trainer.

Development/History

The Cheetah is a redesigned and upgraded version of the Dassault Mirage. Similar in appearance to the IAI Kfir, the existence of the Cheetah was first revealed in 1987. Approximately 23 existing single-seat Mirage III-EZ, RZ and two-seat R2Z are being converted. This involves replacing some 50 per cent of the airframe and fitting the more powerful Atar 9K-50 instead of the 9C. Modifications include canards fitted just aft of the air intakes, strakes are being added under the nose and refinements made to the wing leading edge. The avionics are also being substantially upgraded and ECM equipment added. It will be compatible with the Armscor V3B and V3B AAMs.

Specification

Powerplant
1 x Atar (SNECMA) 9K-50 turbojet.
Power: 49.2 kN (11,055 lb st) dry, 70.6 kN (15,873 lb) with afterburning.

Dimensions
Length: 15.55 m (51 ft)
Span: 8.22 m (26 ft 11 ins)
Height: 4.5 m (14 ft 9 ins)

Weights
Empty: 6,600 kg (14,440 lb)
Max T/O: 13,700 kg (30,200 lb)

Performance
Max Speed: Mach 2.2
Range: Not available.

Armament
2 x 30 mm gun plus V3B/V3C Vukri AAMs or bomb or rockets.

Status
Undergoing conversion

Customers
South Africa

Manufacturer
Atlas - South Africa

Left: The South African air force Atlas Cheetah.

(Atlas)

Atlas Cheetah (South Africa)

Variants

Cheetah EZ: Modification of Mirage EZ.

Cheetah RZ: Modification of Mirage RZ

Cheetah ACW (Advanced Combat Wing): Modifications to the wing resulted in an increase in maximum weight by 600 kg (1,323 lb), increased fuel capacity and increased sustained turn rate by 14 per cent.

Left and right:
The South African air force Atlas Cheetah.
(Jeremy Flack)

Saab Draken (Sweden)

Type: Single-seat fighter, reconnaissance and two-seat operational trainer.

Development/History

The Draken (Dragon) was initially designed in the late 1940s to intercept bombers, but the unusual double-delta shaped aircraft was later developed for a variety of other roles. Initial aerodynamic flight trials were undertaken by the 7/10th scale Saab 210. Three prototypes were ordered and the first flight was made on 25 October 1955. The J-35A Draken entered service with the Swedish air force in March 1960. Designed to just exceed the speed of sound it did not take long to discover that the single Avon engine could actually power the Draken up to Mach 2.

Nearly 550 Drakens had been delivered to the Swedish air force by the time the last aircraft was built. Most have been retired, but the F10 Wing J-35Fs are undergoing an extensive update to enable them to remain operational until 1999 when they will be replaced by the Gripen.

Specification for Draken 35X

Powerplant
1 x Volvo Flygmotor RM-6C turbojet (licence built Rolls Royce Avon 300)
Power: 5,800 kg (12,790 lb st) dry, 8,000 kg (17,650 lb st) with afterburner.

Dimensions
Length: 5.35 m (50 ft 4 ins)
Span: 9.40 m (30 ft 10 ins)
Height: 3.89 m (12 ft 9 ins)

Swedish air force Saab J-35F Draken armed with Rb24 (AIM-9 Sidewinder) and Rb27 (AIM-4 Falcon) AAMs.
(Jeremy Flack)

Weights
Empty:
Max T/O: 15,000 kg (33,070 lb)

Performance
Max Speed: Mach 2 at altitude.
Range: 3,250 km (2,020 miles)

Armament
2 x 30 mm cannon plus nine external attachment points. Typical load can be four AIM-9 Sidewinder (Swedish air force designation Rb24) or AIM-4 Falcon (Rb27). Alternatively a range of rocket pods, bombs and drop tanks can be fitted.

Status
Production complete.

Operators
Austria (J35Ö), Denmark (F-35/RF-35/TF-35), Finland (BS/CS/FS/XS), Sweden (A/B/D/F/SK-35C/S-35E).

Manufacturer
Saab - Sweden

90

Swedish air force J-35F Draken armed with Rb27 (AIM-4 Falcon) missiles.

(Saab via API)

Saab Draken (Sweden)

Variants

J-35: Prototype.
J-35A: Initial production model.
J-35B: Modified J-35A and new build model with S7 fire-control radar.
Sk-35C: Converted J-35A to two-seat operational trainer.
J-35D: J-35B with RM6C/Avon 300 engine plus improved avionics and fuel capacity.
S-35E: Single-seat reconnaissance model similar to J-35D.
J-35F: J-35D with improved weapons and delivery system, afterburner, fuel capacity as well as other avionics.
J-35H: Modified J-35A to try to secure Swiss order.
J-35J: Extensively modified J-35F, includes extra two attachment points plus avionics upgrade.
35X: Long-range multi-purpose export model similar to F-35F with greatly increased attack capability.

A-35XD: Export model of 35X for Denmark. Designated F-35 in service.
S-35XD: Armed reconnaissance export model, designated RF-35 in service.
Sk.35XD: Combat capable two-seat trainer model of A-35XD, designated TF-35 in service.
35E: Modified J-35D for export.
F-35: In-service designation of A-35XD.
RF-35: In-service designation of S-35XD.
TF-35: In-service designation of Sk-35XD.
J-35BS: Ex SwAF model J-35B with all-weather avionics for export.
J-35CS: Ex SwAF model Sk-35C for export.
J-35FS: Ex SwAF model J-35FS for export.
J-35XS: Export model similar to J-35F with additional cannon but not Falcon AAM compatible.

Saab JAS.39 Gripen (Sweden)

Type: Single-seat all-weather, all-altitude interceptor, attack and reconnaissance aircraft.

Development/History

The Gripen programme began in 1980 and an initial development contract for five prototypes and 30 production aircraft was placed in 1982. The prototype Gripen first took to the air on 9 December 1988 and the first production aircraft was flown four years later. Software difficulties affecting the fly-by-wire system, causing the loss of the first prototype and the second production aircraft. This took some time to be resolved but by 1998 some 50 JAS.39 Gripens had been delivered from the 204 aircraft ordered. The total includes 28 of the two-seat trainer variant.

Specification

Powerplant

1 x General Electric/Volvo Flygmotor RM12 (F404-GE-400) turbofan.
Power: Initially 54 kN (12,140 lb st) dry, 80.5 kN (18,100 lb st) with afterburner.

Dimensions

Length: 14.10 m (46 ft 3 ins)
Span: 8.40 m (27 ft 6 3/4 ins)
Height: 4.50 m (14 ft 9 ins)

Weights

Empty: 6,622 kg (14,600 lb)
Max T/O: 13,000 kg (28,600 lb) approx

Performance

Max Speed: Supersonic at all levels.
Range: Combat radius 800 km (497 miles)

Armament

1 x 27 mm cannon (not fitted on JAS.39B) plus seven external stores positions. Those on the wing tips are for Rb74 (AIM-9L) Sidewinder AAMs. The other positions can accommodate additional Rb74s, Mica or AIM-120 AMRAAM AAMs, Rb75 Maverick ASM or RBS-15F anti shipping missile or a range of bombs, rocket pods and drop tanks.

Status

In production.

Customers

Sweden

Manufacturer

Saab - Sweden

Left: BAe Meteor and MRAAM mockups of AAMs on a plastic replica of the Gripen. The Meteor has been designed to meet the FMRAAM (Future Medium Range AAM) programme for the next generation AAM.

Saab JAS.39 Gripen (Sweden)

Ground-crew re-arm a JAS.39 Gripen with SkyFlash AAMs.
(Lindahl/Saab via API)

Variants

JAS.39A: Standard single-seat model.

JAS.39B (Gripen SK): Combat-capable, two-seat training and tactical conversion model.

JAS.39C: Allocated for improved JAS.39A model.

JAS.39D: Allocated for improved JAS.39B model.

JAS.39X: Proposed future export model to JAS.39C/D standard.

Saab Viggen (Sweden)

Type: Single-seat all-weather multi-purpose combat aircraft

Development/History

The Viggen (Thunderbolt) was designed to fulfil four primary roles: attack, interceptor, reconnaissance and training. These were integral components of the Swedish air force System 37 which forms a vital part of their defence system. The first of seven prototypes took to the air on 8 February 1967. Such is the performance of the Viggen that it is capable of operating from narrow, straight stretches of roads about 500 m (1,640 ft) long. Initial deliveries made to the Swedish air force to replace A-32A Lansen from mid 1971. The final delivery in 1990 brought the total built to 329 of all models.

Rb71 (SkyFlash) AAMs on Swedish air force JA-37 Viggen.
(Saab via API)

Specification

Powerplant
1 x Volvo Flygmotor RM8B turbofan
Power: 72.1 kN (16,203 lb st) dry, 125 kN (28,108 lb st) with afterburning.

Dimensions
Length: 16.40 m (53 ft 9 3/4 ins)
Span: 10.60 m (34 ft 9 1/4 ins)
Height: 5.90 m (19 ft 4 1/4 ins)

Weights
Empty: 11,800 kg (26,014 lb)
Max T/O: 17,000 kg (37,478 lb)

Performance
Max Speed: Mach 2+ at altitude.
Range: 2,000 km (1,240 miles)

Armament
1 x 30 mm cannon in permanent belly pack plus seven external attachment points. Typically, six AIM-9L Sidewinder (Swedish air force designation Rb74) plus two Sky Flash (Rb71). Alternatively a range of ASMs, rocket pods, bombs, drop tanks or other pod systems.

Status
Production complete.

Customers
Sweden

Manufacturer
Saab - Sweden

Saab Viggen (Sweden)

Variants

AJ-37: Single-seat attack model with secondary interceptor role.

SF-37: Single-seat armed reconnaissance model.

SH-37: Single-seat all-weather armed sea surveillance model.

Sk-37: Two-seat training model.

JA-37: Single-seat interceptor with improved RM8B engine. A recognition feature is the taller Sk-37 type tail fin.

AJS: Modification of AJ, SF and SH models to an interchangeable model by including all mission capabilities in one system.

Left: JA-37 Viggen with Rb74 (AIM-9 Sidewinder) and Rb71 (SkyFlash) AAMs.

(Saab via API)

Right: Rb74 (AIM-9 Sidewinder) and Rb71 (SkyFlash) AAMs on Swedish air force JA-37 Viggen.

(Jeremy Flack)

Saab Viggen (Sweden)

JA-37 Viggen with Rb74 (AIM-9 Sidewinder) and Rb71 (SkyFlash) AAMs.

(Saab via API)

AIDC Ching-Kuo (Taiwan)

Type: Single-seat air superiority fighter.

Development/History

The programme for the IDF (Indigenous Defensive Fighter) commenced in 1982 following the US Government's refusal to approve the sale of the Northrop F-20 Tigershark or the F-16 to replace Taiwan's fleet of ageing F-104 Starfighters. Development assistance has been provided by General Dynamics, Garrett and Westinghouse for airframe, engine and radar systems respectively. The design was frozen in 1985 and construction of four prototypes commenced. The first made its maiden flight on 28 May 1989. These were followed by a pre-production batch of an additional 10 aircraft. With an original requirement for 250 aircraft, the

Production of the Ching-Kuo is well underway.

Specification

Powerplant

2 x ITEC (AlliedSignal/AIDC) TFE1042-70 (F125) turbofans
Power: 26.8 kN (6,025 lb st) dry, 41.8 kN (9,400 lb st) with afterburner.

Dimensions

Length: 14.21 m (46 ft 7 1/2 ins) including probe
Span: 9.46 m (31 ft 0 1/2 ins) including missiles
Height: 4.65 m (15 ft 3 ins)

Weights

Empty: 6,486 kg (14,300 lb)
Max T/O: 12,247 kg (27,000 lb)

Performance

Max Speed: 1,296 km/h (805 mph) at altitude.
Range: Not available.

Armament

1 x 20mm cannon plus six external attachment points. Typical load is a Sky Sword (TC-1) short range AAM on each wingtip plus a pair under each wing. An additional pair of medium range Sky Sword 2 (TC-2) AAMs can be fitted under the fuselage. Other weaponry includes various combinations of bombs, missiles and rockets plus drop tanks.

Status In production.

Customers

Taiwan

Manufacturer

Aero Industry Development Centre (AIDC) - Taiwan

AIDC Ching-Kuo (Taiwan)

Republic of China air force took delivery of the first production Ching-Kuo in January 1994 but by this time the order had been reduced to 130 aircraft.

Variants
Single-seat: Basic fighter variant.
Two-seat: Advanced conversion trainer.

Two-seat model of the Ching-Kuo.

BAe Hawk 200 (UK)

Type: Single-seat multi-role combat aircraft

Development/History

The Hawk 200 evolved from the current two-seat Hawk trainer with a revised nose and retains an 80 per cent airframe commonalty. Intention to build the Hawk 200 to compliment the family of advanced trainer and attack aircraft was announced in June 1984. The prototype took to the air for the first time on 19 May 1986, but was lost less than two months later. The first production Hawk 200 flew in April 1987.

Variants

T.1: Initial advanced trainer model.

T.1A: Upgrade of T.1 to enable air defence capability with ability to carry two AIM-9 Sidewinders on previously unused hardpoints.

T.1W: Re-winged T.1 model capable of carrying under-wing

Specification for Hawk 200

Powerplant

1 x Rolls Royce Turbomeca Adour Mk.871 turbofan.
Power: 26.0 kN (5,845 lb st) dry.

Dimensions RDA model

Length: 10.99 m (36 ft 0 3/4 ins)
Span: 11.38 m (37 ft 4 ins)
Height: 3.98 m (13 ft 0 3/4 ins)

Weights

Empty: 4,450 kg (9,810 lb)
Max T/O: 9,100 kg (20,061 lb)

Performance

Max Level Speed: 1,000 km/h (621 mph) at sea level.
Range: 2,528 km (1,570 miles) ferry with 2 drop tanks.

Armament

Four external attachment points capable of total of 3,493 kg of stores. These can include AIM-9 Sidewinder AAMs and drop tanks.

Status In production

Customers

Abu Dhabi (63, 63A, 63B, 63C), Dubai (61), Finland (51, 51A), Indonesia (53,109,209), Kenya (52), South Korea (67), Kuwait (64), Malaysia (108, 208), Oman (103, 203), Saudi Arabia (65, 65A), Switzerland (66), UK (T.1, T.1A, T.1W), USA (T-45A, T-45C), Zimbabwe (60, 60A)

Manufacturer

British Aerospace (BAe) - UK

Left: Hawk 200 with ASRAAM. The AIM-132 ASRAAM (Advanced Short Range AAM) has been designed to meet the RAF need for a new short range missile. With a range of 10 km it will initially replace the Sidewinder of the Harrier GR.7 and eventually become part of the Eurofighter inventory. It is capable of hitting a target 90 degrees off boresight.

(Jeremy Flack)

BAe Hawk 200 armed with a pair of AIM-9 Sidewinder AAMs.

BAe Sea Harrier FA. Mk2 (UK)

Type: Single-seat, V/STOL fighter, reconnaissance and attack aircraft.

Development/History

The Sea Harrier is a naval variant of the RAF Harrier close support aircraft. Development of the Sea Harrier involved a revised forward fuselage to provide capacity for the Blue Fox radar and give the pilot improved all round visibility. The first Sea Harrier took to the air on 20 August 1978. Initial deliveries to the Royal Navy commenced the following June. In 1982 the Sea Harrier was deployed operationally in the Falklands war. A total of 29 FRS. Mk1s were deployed and flew 2,376 sorties; 22 Argentine aircraft were destroyed by the Sea Harriers without any loss, although four Sea Harriers were lost in accidents and two to ground fire.

India took strong interest in the Sea Harrier for its navy,

RN Sea Harrier FA. Mk2 takes off armed with an AMRAAM AAM. (Jeremy Flack)

Specification Harrier FA. Mk2

Powerplant
1 x Rolls Royce Pixies Mk.104 vectored thrust turbofan.
Power: 95.6 kN (21,500 lb st) dry.

Dimensions
Length: 14.17 m (46 ft 6 ins)
Span: 7.70m (23 ft 3 ins)
Height: 3.61 m (11 ft 10 ins)

Weights
Empty: 6,374 kg (14,052 lb)
Max T/O: 11,880 kg (26,200 lb)

Performance
Max Level Speed: 1,185 km/h (736 mph) at low level.
Range: 1,500 km (932 miles)

Armament
Seven external attachment positions capable of up to 3,630 kg (8,000 lb) of stores. Typical load is four AIM-120B AMRAAM missiles. One on each of the two outer positions and a pair under the fuselage. A pair of drop tanks would also be located on the inner wing points. A pair of 30 mm cannons can be fitted under the fuselage replacing the two strike farings. Alternatively, AIM-9 Sidewinder AAMs can be carried or various bombs and rocket pods.

Status
No longer in production.

Customers
India (FRS.51/T.60), UK (FRS.1/FA.2/T.4N/T.8N)

Manufacturer
British Aerospace (BAe) - UK

BAe Sea Harrier FA. Mk2 (UK)

Below: The Hughes AIM-120 AMRAAM (Advanced Medium Range AAM) is a BVR (Beyond Visual Range) missile capable of hitting an enemy aircraft at ranges in excess of 48 km (30 miles). Seen here on a Royal Navy Sea Harrier FA. Mk2, the AMRAAM has notched up three kills, two during the Gulf War and one during a patrol over Bosnia.

(Jeremy Flack)

resulting in the order of 23 FRS. Mk 51 and four T.60. They also purchased the Falklands veteran carrier, HMS *Hermes*, which was re-named INS *Viraat*. A discussion to upgrade these aircraft commenced in 1994 which included to possible installation of Blue Vixen radar but has yet to be finalised.

The Sea Harrier FA. Mk2 was the result of a mid-life upgrade to the Sea Harrier FRS. Mk1 which entered a project definition stage in 1985. The main visual difference is the larger diameter radome to house the Blue Vixen radar. Other upgrades include increased missile launch ranges and enhanced surface target acquisition. An ability to track multiple targets and the capability to operate the AIM-120B AMRAAM AAM combine to make the Sea Harrier FA.2 an effective fighter.

First FA Mk.2 conversion flew on 19 September 1988 and all surviving 33 FRS.Mk1s converted plus the prototypes and first production aircraft that were later subject to return for full conversion. Orders were also placed for 18 new FA. Mk2s.

Royal Navy Sea Harrier FA. Mk2 on HMS Illustrious equipped with Sidewinder training rounds.

(Jeremy Flack)

Royal Navy Sea Harrier FA. Mk2s on HMS Invincible armed with AIM-9 Sidewinder AAMs.

(Jeremy Flack)

BAe Sea Harrier FA. Mk2 (UK)

Variants

FRS. Mk1: Initial production model.

FRS. Mk51: Export model.

FRS. Mk2: Initial designation for FA.2.

FA. Mk2: Modified FRS.1 with Blue Vixen radar and AMRAAM compatible.

T.4N: Two-seat conversion trainer modified from RAF T.4N.

T.8N: Two-seat conversion trainer compatible with FA.2.

Left: RN Sea Harrier hovering over HMS Invincible armed with AIM-9 Sidewinder AAMs.
(Jeremy Flack)

Right: Indian Navy Sea Harrier FRS. Mk51 hovering. (Jeremy Flack)

Grumman F-14 Tomcat (USA)

Type: Carrier-borne two-seat area air-defence and multi-role fighter.

Development/History

Grumman gained considerable experience from the cancelled F-111B development programme. In January 1969, this resulted in its successful G-303 submission to the US Navy for its still unresolved requirement for a multi-role fighter. The prototype YF-14A first took to the air on 21 December 1970. Sadly it was lost a few days later on its second flight due to a hydraulic failure on landing. Despite this setback the development proceeded well and orders followed.

Initial deliveries were made to the US Navy in 1972, with an eventual total of 557 F-14As which were used to establish up to 30 squadrons. A further 38 F-14Bs were delivered and 32 F-14As were modified with F110 engines to bring them up to F-14B standard. An anticipated order of some 400 F-14Ds was reduced down to just 37 aircraft together with a few updated earlier models.

Specification F-14D Tomcat

Powerplant
2 x General Electric F110-GE-400 turbofans.
Power: 71.56 kN (16,088 lb st) dry, 120.1 kN (27,000 lb st) with afterburner.

Dimensions
Length: 18.87 m (61 ft 11 ins)
Span: 19.56 m (64 ft 2 ins) spread
             11.63 m (38 ft 2 ins) swept
Height: 4.88 m (16 ft 0 ins)

Weights
Empty: 18,951 kg (41,780 lb)
Max T/O: 33,724 kg (74,349 lb)

Performance
Max Speed: Mach 1.88 at altitude
Range: 2,965 km (1,842 miles)

Armament
1 x 20 mm cannon plus six external stores stations totalling 6,577 kg (14,500 lb). Typical load is four AIM-54 Phoenix under the fuselage plus two AIM-9 Sidewinder and two AIM-7 Sparrow AAMs under the wings to give an effective close, medium and BVR capability. Alternative permutations can be carried according to the mission. In addition the F-14 has the capability to deliver bombs.

Status
No longer in production.

Customers
Iran, USA.

Manufacturer
Grumman - USA

Left: A USN F-14 Tomcat launches an AIM-54 Phoenix at a target that could be over 200 km (124 miles) away.
(Hughes via API)

The swept wings provide a more efficient high speed wing shape.

(Grumman via API)

Grumman F-14 Tomcat (USA)

Variants

YF-14A: Prototype

YF-14B: Re-engined trials aircraft with P&W F401 engine.

F-14A: Initial production model.

F-14B: Retrofitted F-14As with F110 engine (also referred to as F-14A plus) plus some system changes.

F-14C: Proposed F-14A with enhanced avionics and weapons.

F-14D: Enhanced F-14B with improved radar and avionics.

JF-14A: One off F-14A modified for trials duties.

NF-14D: Three F-14Ds for trials duties

Right: Wings are swept forward ready for launching.
(Jeremy Flack)

Above and right: Wings are kept swept to reduce space to a minimum.

(Jeremy Flack)

110

Above: The AIM-54 Phoenix AAM gives the Tomcat an excellent BVR (Beyond Visual Range) capability with a 200+ km (124 miles) range.

(Jeremy Flack)

Right: AIM-7 Sparrow and AIM-54 Phoenix AAMs are brought up from below deck for loading when the Tomcat is prepared for flight.

(Jeremy Flack)

Lockheed F-104 Starfighter (USA)

Type: Single-seat interceptor and multi-role fighter.

Development/History

The Starfighter was originally conceived in 1953 following exhaustive research by famous designer CL 'Kelly' Johnson. Built as a lightweight high-speed fighter, the prototype XF-104 first flew on 4 March 1954. Some 50 of the initial production models were allocated to the development and trials which were fraught with difficulties. Acceptance by the USAF was given in 1958 but the F-104As were temporarily grounded three months later and in the following year they were transferred to the ANG. The much improved F-104C was already in production by this time and deliveries commenced to the USAF. This proved to be a far more acceptable fighter and remained on front-line service until 1965.

The emergence of the F-104G as a multi-role fighter aided by a controversial marketing strategy achieved major export orders in Europe. Such was the demand that

Close-up of the gun bay of the F-104G Starfighter.
(Jeremy Flack)

Specification

Powerplant

1 x General Electric J79-GE-19 turbojet
Power: 52.8 kN (11,870 lb st) dry, 79.62 kN (17,900 lb) with afterburner.

Dimensions

Length: 16.69 m (54 ft 9 ins)
Span: 6.68 m (21 ft 11 ins)
Height: 4.15 m (13 ft 6 ins)

Weights

Empty: 6,700 kg (14,900 lb)
Max T/O: 14,060 kg (31,000 lb)

Performance

Max Speed: Mach 2.2 at altitude.
Range: 2,920 km (1,815 miles)

Armament

1 x 20 mm cannon plus up to nine external attachment points. Typical configuration is a Sidewinder on each wing tip plus a Sparrow or Aspide AAMs under each wing or a range of AGMs, bombs or drop tanks.

Status

Production complete.

Customers

Belgium (D/G), Canada (CF-104D/G), Denmark (D/G), Germany (D/G/RF), Greece (G), Italy (D/G/S), Japan (DJ/J), Jordan (A/B), Netherlands (D/G/RF), Norway (D/G), Pakistan (A/B), Spain (D/G), Taiwan (D/G/RF) Turkey (D/G/S), USA (A/B/C/D).

Manufacturer

Lockheed - USA
Canadair - Canada
MBB - Germany
Aeritalia - Italy
SABCA - Netherlands
Mitsubishi - Japan

Lockheed F-104 Starfighter (USA)

collaborative licence production lines were established in various European countries and Japan. Now superseded by the F-16, the only significant user of the Starfighter today is the Italian air force, which developed the F-104S to accommodate the AIM-7 Sparrow instead of the usual Sidewinder. The F-104S visibly differs from other variants with an additional pair of strakes under the rear fuselage. A total of 246 F-104S were built when production was completed in 1979.

Above: German navy F-104G Starfighter armed with AIM-9 Sidewinder AAM.

(Jeremy Flack)

Left: Lockheed F-104G Starfighter cockpit.

(Jeremy Flack)

Variants

XF-104: Prototype.

YF-104: Pre-production model.

F-104A: Initial production model.

F-104B: Two-seat trainer F-104A.

F-104C: Improved F-104A model

F-104D: Two-seat trainer of F-104C.

F-104G: Multi-role export model.

F-104S: Improved F-104G optimised for air defence.

CF-104: Re-engined F-104C with Orenda J79-OEL-7 and optimised for close-air-support (CAS) without internal gun.

RF-104G: Reconnaissance model of F-104G with camera pack replacing gun.

F-104J: Similar to F-104G but optimised as interceptor.

QF-104: Converted F-104A/B for use as unmanned target drones.

F-104N: Used for astronaut training.

Above: German navy F-104G Starfighter armed with AIM-9 Sidewinder AAM and Kormoran anti-shipping missile.

(Jeremy Flack)

Left: The largest current Starfighter operator is the Italian air force with the F-104S model.

(Jeremy Flack)

115

Lockheed Martin F-16 Fighting Falcon (USA)

Type: Single-seat multi-role fighter and two-seat conversion trainer.

Development/History

The F-16 was the successful contender for the USAF Lightweight Fighter programme of 1972. The first prototype, designated YF-16, first took to the air on 2 February 1974. In 1975 it was selected for full-scale development and an air-to-ground capability including radar and all-weather navigation was added to the original purely day fighter requirement. The first production F-16A took to the air on 7 August 1978 and entered service with 388th TFW at Hill AFB five months later. Operational Capabilities Upgrade (OCU) upgrade to the F-16 comprised an international programme to prepare the aircraft in readiness for the AMRAAM missile. In 1991 an engine upgrade was starting to be implemented replacing the F100-PW-200 with the F100-PW-220E. A Mid-Life Update (MLU) was agreed in 1993 for European operators to have an F-16C style cockpit with a wide angle HUD and night vision capability together with improvements to various avionic systems. The implementation of the Multinational Staged Improvement Programme (MSIP) in 1980 resulted in the F-16C/D enabling subsequent upgrades to be easily incorporated.

The next improvements to the F-16 were undertaken in production batches. Block 40/42 aircraft were also referred to as the 'Night Falcon' as they were fully compatible with the Low-Altitude Navigation and Targeting Infra-Red for Night (LANTIRN) pods. In addition there were various improvements to the avionics, structure, EW capability and weapon delivery systems. Block 50/52 gave an optional engine (F110-PB-129/229) with improved performance as well as radar, communications and radar warning

Specification F-16C Block 50

Powerplant
1 x General Electric F110-GE-129 or Pratt & Whitney F100-PW-229 turbofan.
Power: 131.6 kN (29,588 lb st) dry or 129.4 kN (29,100 lb st) with afterburner.

Dimensions
Length: 15.05 m (49 ft 4 ins)
Span: 10.0 m (31 ft 0 ins) over missiles
Height: 5.09 m (16 ft 8 1/2 ins)

Weights
Empty: 8,581 kg (18,917 lb)
Max T/O: 12,292 kg (27,099 lb)

Performance
Max Speed: Mach 2.0+ above 12,200 m (40,000 ft)
Range: 4,215 km (2,634 miles) ferry with 1500 US gal drop tanks.

Armament
1 x 20 mm cannon plus nine external attachment points for total of 9,278 kg for 5.5 g manoeuvring or 5,420 kg for 9 g. Typical load would be six AIM-9 Sidewinder or AMRAAM AAMs plus drop tanks. Alternative load can include Python 3, Sparrow, Sky Flash, ASRAAM or Magic 2 AAMs, Maverick AGM, TAAS Star 1, HARM or Shrike ARM, Penguin 3 or Harpoon anti-ship missile plus a range of bombs, rocket pods and drop tanks. A further two mounting provisions are located on either side of the inlet shoulder specifically for FLIR/LANTIRN type pods.

Status
In production

Operators
Bahrain (C/D) Belgium (A/B), Denmark (A/B), Egypt (A/B/C/D), Greece (C/D), Indonesia (A/B), Israel (A/B/C/D), Jordan (A/B), South Korea (C/D), Netherlands (A/B), Norway (A/B), Pakistan (A/B), Portugal (A/B), Singapore (A/B/C/D), Taiwan (A/B), Thailand (A/B), Turkey (C/D), USA (A/B/C/D/N), Venezuela (A/B).

Manufacturer
Lockheed Martin (formerly General Dynamics) - USA
Samsung - South Korea

F-16D of the Bahrain Amiri air force.

Lockheed Martin F-16 Fighting Falcon (USA)

enhancements. Block 50D/52D fully integrated the HARM/Shrike anti-radar missile (ARM) with the F-16

Numerous modification programs have improved the F-16 over the years. While many have not changed the designation, some have been for a specific role. The F-16A(ADF) was intended as a F-4 Phantom/F-106 Delta Dart interceptor replacement for the air defence units of the Air National Guard (ANG). The modifications included a radar upgrade to improve small target acquisition as well as permitting it to operate the AIM-7 Sparrow and AIM-120 AMRAAM AAMs. A total of 226 F-16As and 25 F-16Bs were modified but with end of the Cold War many have been withdrawn and replaced by surplus front-line F-16Cs.

Various upgrade proposals are under consideration today.

One proposal is to modify some 300 block 30/32 F-16Cs specifically to the close air support/battlefield air interdiction role. Another is to convert surplus stored aircraft into the F-16/UCAV by the removal of cockpit and other life support systems and increase fuel plus the addition of long wings to enable safe attacks against highly defended targets.

Variants
YF-16: Prototype
F-16A: Initial production model
F-16A(R): Modified F-16A of Royal Netherlands air force to carry Oude Delft Orpheus reconnaissance pod.
F-16B: Two-seat trainer

Above: USAF F-16A firing an AMRAAM during trials.
(Jeremy Flack)

Right: This F-16(ADF) is operated by the Illinois ANG and can be identified by the four small spade aerials just in front of the cockpit.
(Jeremy Flack)

118

Egyptian air force F-16A

(General Dynamics via API)

Lockheed Martin F-16 Fighting Falcon (USA)

F-16B-2: F-16/79 with F100 engine used for weapon delivery systems evaluation.

F-16C: Multinational Staged Improvement Programme model.

F-16ES: Modified F-16C as Enhanced Strategic two-seat long-range interceptor proposal.

F-16N: Modified F-16C for unarmed supersonic adversary aircraft role.

TF-16N: Modified F-16D for unarmed supersonic adversary aircraft role.

F-16U: Proposed two-seat interdictor with range greater than F-16ES and fitted with delta wing.

F-16X: Proposed development with 1.42 m stretched and F-22 type wing.

ATFI/F-16: Modified pre-series F-16A for research and fitted with chin mounted canard winglets. Sub variants = DFCS - Digital Flights Control System; AMAS - Automated Manoeuvre Attack System; CAS - Close Air Support.

F-16/79: Second pre-series F-16B used for alternative J-79 engine development.

F-16/101: Pre-series F-16A used for alternative F101 engine development.

Falcon 2000: Proposed model similar to F-16U as JSF back-up should the problem delay the programme.

GF-16A: Time expired F-16A airframes used for ground training.

GF-16B: Time expired F-16B airframes used for ground training.

GF-16C: Time expired F-16C airframes used for ground training.

In this configuration the F-16 is fitted with four AIM-120 AMRAAM and a pair of LGBs (Laser Guided Bombs) for the ground attack role. (Jeremy Flack)

F-16(ADF): Modified F-16A. Recognition feature are the four small aerials just in front of the cockpit.
Block 40/42 Night Falcon: Improvements include fully compatible with LANTIRN day/night stand-off target identification system.
Block 50/52: Enhanced engine and avionics and HARM ARM compatible.
Block 50+: Projected model with advanced avionics for JDAM compatibility plus increased drop tank capability.
Block 60/62: Projected development similar to F-16ES.
NF-16D: Variable-Stability In-Flight Simulator Test Aircraft (VISTA).
F-16XL: Modified pre-series F-16As to incorporate cranked or double-delta wing similar to SAAB Draken.
Model 1600/1601/1602: LTV proposed naval F-16 model lost out to twin engined F/A-18 Hornet.
F-16/UCAV: Proposed conversion of F-16A to Unmanned Combat Aerial Vehicle to fly long endurance stand off weapons.
FSX/F-2: Mitsubishi developed aircraft evolved from the F-16C but with larger redesigned composite wings. (See Mitsubishi F-2 entry).

A USAF F-16C of 52nd FW armed with a pair of AIM-120 AMRAAM and a pair of AIM-9 Sidewinder AAMs during a mission over Bosnia.

(Jeremy Flack)

121

Lockheed Martin F-22 Raptor (USA)

Type: Single seat air superiority fighter with air-to-surface capability.

Development/History

The F-22 was designed to meet a USAF requirement for 750 new fighters to replace the F-15 Eagle, an order later reduced to 442. Initially referred to as the Advanced Tactical Fighter (ATF), the F-22 incorporates low observable technology together with supercruise capability (supersonic speeds without need for afterburner).

Initial work commenced in the early 1980s with definition contracts issued in 1983. Competition selection resulted in orders for two flying demonstration prototypes and one static example of the YF-22 and Northrop YF-23. The first YF-22 took to the air on 29 September 1990. In April 1989 the F-22 was declared to be the winner and 11 prototypes were ordered, including a pair of F-22B two-seat trainers. These were subsequently reduced to nine in 1998 after the cancellation of the F-22B. In 1993 it was decided to add an air-to-ground attack role using precision-guided munitions. As a result the weapons bay and the avionics were modified to be able to accept AIM-9X and JDAM (500 kg GBU-32). Prototypes are currently in production and the first production F-22 is expected to be delivered in March 2002.

Variants

645: Lockheed project number.
YF-22: Prototype.
F-22A: Production model.
F-22B: Cancelled two-seat conversion trainer
NATF: Naval model to replace F-14, project abandoned.

Specification

Powerplant
2 x Pratt & Whitney F119-PW-100 advanced technology turbofans.
Power: 155 kN (35,000 lb st)

Dimensions
Length: 18.92 m (62 ft 1 ins)
Span: 13.56 m (44 ft 6 ins)
Height: 5.05 m (16 ft 7 ins)
Weights
Empty: 14,365 kg (31,670 lb) target
Max T/O: 27,216 kg (60,000 lb)

Performance
Max Speed: 1,482 km/h (921 mph)
Range: Not available.

Status
In production

Right and far right: The Lockheed Martin F-22 is now undergoing extensive flight development before it enters service in 2002.
(Lockheed Martin via API)

Customers
USA

Manufacturer
Boeing (formerly Lockheed Martin) - USA

McDonnell Douglas F-4 Phantom (USA)

Type: Two-seat multi-role fighter

Development/History

The F-4 Phantom was designed to meet a 1955 US Navy requirement for a long-range all-weather attack fighter. The prototype XF4H-1H was first flown on 27 May 1958. The Phantom was soon to catch much attention when an active policy of record-breaking was pursued with unmodified aircraft.

The first Phantoms entered service with the USN in 1961. The USAF ordered substantial numbers too, and when the final Phantom was completed in Japan in 1981 a total of 5,195 had been built. Some 117 F-4E Phantoms were

German air force F-4F Phantom

Specification F-4B

Powerplant

2 x General Electric J79-GE-8 turbojet.
Power: 48.5 kN (10,900 lb st) dry, 75.6 kN (17,000 lb st) with afterburner.

Dimensions

Length: 17.76 m (58 ft 3 ins)
Span: 11.70 m (38 ft 5 ins)
Height: 4.96 m (16 ft 3 ins)

Weights

Empty: 12,700 kg (28,000 lb)
Max T/O: 24,765 kg (54,600 lb)

Performance

Max Speed: Mach 2+ at altitude.
Range: 3,700 km (2,300 miles) ferry

Armament

Six external attachment points for total load of 7,250 kg (16,000 lb). Typically, four AIM-7 Sparrow and two AIM-9 Sidewinder AAMs plus two drop tanks. Alternatively, a range of AGM, ASM, bombs, rocket pods can be carried.

Status Production complete.

Customers

Germany (F/RF-4E), Greece (E/RF-4E), Iran (D) Israel, Japan (EJ/RF-4EJ), South Korea (D), Spain (C), Turkey, UK (FG.1(K)/FRS.2(M)), USA (A,B,C,D,E)

Manufacturer

McDonnell Douglas - USA
Mitsubishi - Japan

converted to F-4G for the 'Wild Weasel' role locating and destroying enemy radar and SAM sites. They saw extensive use during the Gulf War and remained in the USAF long after most other variants were withdrawn.

Variants

XF4H-1: Prototype.
F-4A: Initial production with J79-GE-2 engines.
F-4B: All-weather fighter for USN/USMC with J79-GE-8.
QF-4B: Converted F-4B to unpiloted target role.

RF-4B: Reconnaissance model of F-4B with cameras in enlarged nose.
F-4C: Developed from F-4B for USAF with J79-GE-15 engines, alternative avionics and boom flight refuelling system.
RF-4C: Tactical reconnaissance model of F-4C with cameras in enlarged nose.
F-4E: Multi-role model with 20 mm internal gun, improved avionics and J79-GE-17 engines.
F-4F: Interceptor model of F-4E with reduced ground attack

Spanish air force RF-4C Phantom.

(Jeremy Flack)

125

McDonnell Douglas F-4 Phantom (USA)

avionics and leading edge slats to increase manoeuvrability.

F-4G: 'Wild Weasel' air defence suppression model converted from F-4E.

F-4J: Development of F-4B with full ground attack capability.

F-4K: Development of F-4B with substantial UK equipment including Rolls Royce Spey engines for Royal navy designated FG.1 in service.

F-4M: Similar to F-4K with larger air intakes designated FGR.2 in service.

F-4N: Modified F-4B

F-4S: Upgraded F-4J with J79-GE-10B and enhanced avionics plus leading edge slats fitted.

Kurnass 2000: Proposed Israeli Phantom upgrade.

Above: German air force F-4F Phantom

Right: Stocks of surplus F-4 Phantoms are stored by AMARC at Davis Monthan AFB

(Jeremy Flack)

RAF Phantom FGR.2 armed with four AIM-9 Sidewinders plus four AIM-7 Sparrow AAMs under the fuselage.   *(Jeremy Flack)*

McDonnell Douglas F-15 Eagle (USA)

Type: Single-seat air-superiority fighter with secondary attack role.

Development/History

The F-15 was selected to meet a new USAF air superiority requirement from a number of designs in 1969 and was awarded a development contract requiring 20 prototypes. The first took to the air on 27 July 1972 and entered service with the USAF in 1974. By 1979 a total of 383 F-15A and 60 F-16B had been delivered when production changed to the improved F-15C/D.

The F-15E Strike Eagle was a further development of the successful F-15C/D involving a 60 per cent structural

A USAF F-15C Eagle launches an AMRAAM AAM. *(Hughes via API)*

Specification F-15A Eagle

Powerplant
2 x Pratt and Whitney F100-PW-220 turbofans.
Power: 66.7 kN (15,000 lb st) dry, 104.3 kN (23,450 lb st) with afterburner.

Dimensions
Length: 19.43 m (63 ft 9 ins)
Span: 13.05 m (42 ft 9 3/4 ins)
Height: 5.63 m (18 ft 5 1/2 ins)

Weights
Empty: 12,973 kg (28,600 lb)
Max T/O: 30,845 kg (68,000 lb)

Performance
Max Speed: Mach 2.5+ at altitude.
Range: 5,745 km (3,570 miles) ferry with max fuel.

Armament
1 x 20 mm gun plus 11 external attachment points. Typically these can include four AIM-9L/M Sidewinder and four AIM-7F/M Sparrow or eight AMRAAM AAMs. When fitted with conformal fuel tanks up to 10,705 kg (23,600 lb) of bombs can be carried.

Status In production.

Customers
Israel (A/B/C/D), Japan (J/DJ), Saudi Arabia (C/D/S), USA (A/B/C/D/E).

Manufacturer
McDonnell Douglas - USA
Mitsubishi - Japan

USAF F-15 Eagle shows off its load of four AIM-9 Sidewinder and four AIM-7 Sparrow AAMs.   *(McDonnell Douglas via API)*

McDonnell Douglas F-15 Eagle (USA)

Left: USAF F-15D Eagle of 60th FS, 33rd FW.
(Jeremy Flack)

Right: This USAF F-15 Eagle is armed with four AIM-9 Sidewinder and four AIM-7 Sparrow AAMs. *(USAF via API)*

Below: Iraqi kill markings applied to a USAF F-15 after it destroyed the aircraft in air-to-air combat during the Gulf War.
(Jeremy Flack)

redesign. It incorporated new avionics together with extra fuel located in conformal fuel tanks (CFT). These are fitted along the fuselage, beneath the wing. Together with special weapon attachment equipment it has a large capacity for air-to-ground weapons. Other future roles that have been considered for the F-15C/D are for a 'Wild Weasel' model with HARM missiles and a reconnaissance variant.

Both the USAF F-15C Eagle and F-15E Strike Eagle saw extensive use during the Gulf War which resulted in their destroying 34 Iraqi out of 41 shot down in air combat without any loss to themselves. In addition, a Royal Saudi air force pilot shot down two Iraqi fighters in a single mission. Earlier, in 1974, the Israeli F-15As claimed a total of 56.5 kills.

McDonnell Douglas F-15 Eagle (USA)

Variants

F-15A: Initial production model.

TF-15A: Two-seat trainer prototype later redesignated F-15B.

F-15B: Two-seat operational training model.

F-15C: F-15A capable of taking CFTs.

F-15D: Two-seat trainer model of F-15C.

F-15DJ: Japanese model similar to F-15D.

F-15E: Two-seat attack/air superiority model.

F-15F: Proposed single-seat model of F-15E optimised for air combat.

F-15H: Proposed export model lacking specialised air-to-ground capability.

F-15I: Export model of F-15E specifically for Israel.

F-15J: Japanese model similar to F-15C.

F-15S: Export model of F-15E specifically for Saudi Arabia.

F-15 S/MTD: STOL/Manoeuvring Technology Demonstrator with thrust vectoring.

F-15U: Proposed long-range F-15E for UAE requirement.

F-15U Plus: Further extended range F-15E with redesigned thicker wing and additional external stores stations.

Akef: Israeli name given to F-15C/D model.

Baz: Israeli name given to F-15A/B model.

Above: USAF F-15A Eagles armed with AIM-9 Sidewinder AAM.

(Jeremy Flack)

Right: A USAF F-15C is joined by a RAF Tornado F.3 to escort a Soviet Tu-95 'Bear'.

(Jeremy Flack)

McDonnell Douglas F/A-18 Hornet (USA)

Type: Carrier-borne and land based fighter/attack aircraft

Development/History

Northrop proposed the F-17 to meet a joint USAF/US Navy lightweight fighter requirement but finally lost out on a USAF order to the F-16. The uncommitted USN preferred a multi-mission role and a teamed redesign with McDonnell resulted in an order for 11 prototypes. The first flew on 18 November 1978 and after a successful development delivery of production aircraft commenced two years later. Some 370 F/A-18A and 40 F/A-18B two-seat trainers were built to replace F-4 Phantoms and A-7 Corsairs with US Navy and US Marine Corps, and eventually the A-6 Intruders too.

The improved F/A-18C now features night-attack capable avionics. The Hornet proved useful during Desert Storm when over 10,000 sorties were flown, dropping over 9,000 tons of ordnance. Only one aircraft was lost in combat. During the

Specification for F/A-18C Hornet

Powerplant
2 x General Electric F404-GE-402 turbofans.
Power: 78.3 kN (17,600 lb st) with afterburner.

Dimensions
Length: 17.07 m ((56 ft 0 ins)
Span: 12.31 m (40 ft 4 3/4 ins) over missiles
Height: 4.66 m (15 ft 3 1/2 ins)

Weights
Empty: 10,810 kg (23,832 lb)
Max T/O: 25,401 kg (56,000 lb) approx.

Performance
Max Speed: Mach 1.8+
Range: 3,333 km (2,071 miles) ferry - unrefuelled.

Armament
1 x 6-barrel gun plus nine external stores stations totalling 6,227 kg (13,700 lb) of stores. The wing-tip stations are for AIM-9 Sidewinder AAMs while an assortment of various other missiles, bombs, rockets and special pods can be fitted on the other positions. These can includes additional Sidewinders, AIM-7 Sparrow or AIM-120 AMRAAM AAMs, AGM-84 Harpoon or AGM-65 Maverick AGMs. Drop tanks can be fitted to the centre line and two inboard positions. In addition a pair of nacelle fuselage stations can be used to carry FLIR or other sensor pods or additional Sparrow AAMs.

Status In production

Customers
Australia (A/B), Canada (CF-18A(CF-118A)/CF-5B(CF-118B)), Finland (C/D), Kuwait (C/D), Malaysia (D), Spain (EF-18(F-A/18A), Switzerland (C/D), Thailand (Ordered C/D), USA (A/B/C/D Ordered E/F).

Manufacturer
Boeing (previously McDonnell Douglas) - USA

Left: Spanish air force EF-18As armed with AIM-9 Sidewinder AAMs and AGM-88 HARM and radiation missiles during a mission over Bosnia. *(Jeremy Flack)*

An AIM-120 AMRAAM being launched from the enlarged F/A-18E Super Hornet during its development programme.

(McDonnell Douglas via API)

McDonnell Douglas F/A-18 Hornet (USA)

A USMC F/A-18D Hornet of VFMA(AW)-225. (Jeremy Flack)

Line up of USMC F/A-18As of VFMA(AW)-314. (Jeremy Flack)

final stages of one bombing mission, Iraqi fighters were detected on an intercept course. The pair of F/A-18s switched to intercept mode, locked on and launched AAMs which destroyed the air targets, then reverted to attack role to successfully hit the ground target.

In 1992 a major modification of the Hornet was proposed to replace the cancelled A-12 as well as a follow on for the F/A-18A and other USN/USMC attack aircraft. Designated F/A-18E, it was first flown on 29 November 1995. It is a stretched version of the original design with a 0.86 m (2 ft 10 ins) plug and span increased by 1.31 m (4 ft 4 1/2 ins) with a 40 per cent increased range/payload capability.

Variants
YF-18: Prototype.
F/A-18A: Initial production model.
F/A-18B: Two-seat combat capable trainer model.
F/A-18C: Improved F/A-18A model with AIM-120 AMRAAM and added all-weather capability.
F/A-18D: Two-seat model of F/A-18C. Used by USN in training role and USMC to replace A-6E Intruders, OA-4 Skyhawks in attack role.
F/A-18C: Night Attack Upgraded F/A-18C with all-weather night attack avionics.
F/A-18D: Night Attack Upgraded F/A-18D with all-weather night attack avionics.
F/A-18D(RC): Reconnaissance model of F/A-18D
F/A-18E: Re-designed enlarged Super Hornet.
F/A-18F: Two-seat F/A-18E model.
Australian air force-18A: Export model of F/A-18C

specifically for Australia.

ATF-18A: Export model of F/A-18D specifically for Australia.

CF-18A: Export model of F/A-18A specifically for Canada designated CF-188A in service.

CF-18B: Export model of F/A-18B specifically for Canada designated CF-188B in service.

CF-188A: In service designation for CF-18A.

CF-188B: In service designation for CF-18B.

EF-18A: Export model of F/A-18A specifically for Spain designated C.15 in service.

EF-18B: Export model of F/A-18B specifically for Spain designated CE.15 in service.

C.15: In service designation for EF-18A.

CE.15: In service designation for EF-18B.

TF-18A: Initial designation for F/A-18B.

F/A-18 HARV: High Angle of attack Research Vehicle

Above: Formation of F/A-18Ds of VMFA(AW)-533 of the USMC on patrol over Bosnia.
(Jeremy Flack)

Right: Cockpit of USN F/A-18C Hornet.
(Jeremy Flack)

Northrop F-5 Freedom Fighter/Tiger II (USA)

Type: Single-seat light multi-role fighter

Development/History

Developed to meet a US Government requirement for a lightweight, high-performance fighter which it could supply to friendly nations through the Military Aid Programme, design of the F-5 commenced in 1955. Initially designated N-156, initial US military interest was shown in a two-seat trainer variant designated T-38 Talon which first took to the air on 10 April 1959. The N-156C continued as a private development and the prototype first flew on 30 July 1959. It took until 1962 for the USAF selection of the N-156C to be approved. With the military designation the prototype F-5A was first flown in May 1963 and entered operational service the following year, although it was beaten by the F-5B by four months.

With the F-5A/B in production, Northrop continued development and modified an F-5A into the prototype F-5E which was first flown in March 1969. In 1970 it won the US Government's International Fighter Aircraft competition which was to select a successor to the F-5A/B. In USAF and USN operation the manoeuvrable F-5E is used for aggressor training in which it was flown to represent likely enemy aircraft, especially the MiG-21.

A further development produced the F-20 Tigershark prototypes for a 1986 competition but lost out to the F-16. When production ended in early 1989 a total of 3,805 F-5A/B/C/E/F and T-38s had been built. More recently, various upgrades have proposed and some implemented to extend the life of the F-5.

Specification of F-5E

Powerplant
2 x General Electric J85-GE-21B turbojets
Power: 1,588 kg (3,500 lb st) dry, 2,268 kg (5,000 lb st) with afterburner.

Dimensions
Length: 14.45 m (47 ft 4 ins)
Span: 8.13 m (26 ft 8 ins)
Height: 4.07 m (13 ft 4 ins)

Weights
Empty: 4,410 kg (9,723 lb)
Max T/O: 11,214 kg (24.722 lb)

Performance
Max Speed: Mach 1.64 at altitude.
Range: 3,175 km (1,974 miles)

Armament
2 x 20 mm cannons plus five external attachment points for total of 3,175 kg (7,000 lb) stores. Typical load is am AIM-9 Sidewinder on each wingtip plus a range of rockets pods, bombs and drop tanks.

Status
Production complete.

Customers
Bahrain (E/F), Brazil (E/F), Canada (CF-5A/D), Chile (E/F), Egypt (E/F), Ethiopia (A/B), Greece (A/B), Iran (A/B/E/F), Jordan (E/F), Kenya (E/F), Libya (A/B), South Korea (A/B/E/F), Malaysia (E/F), Morocco (A/B), Netherlands (NF-5A/B), Norway (A/B/G/RF-5G), Philippines (A/B), Saudi Arabia (E/F), Singapore (E/F), Spain (A/B), Sudan (E/F), Switzerland (E/F), Taiwan (A/B/E/F), Thailand (A/B/E/F), USA (A/B/E/F), (Vietnam A/B), Venezuela (CF-5A/D.

Manufacturer
Northrop - USA
Canadair - Canada
Korean Air - Korea
Fokker - Netherlands
AISA (became CASA) - Spain
AIDC - Taiwan

A USMC F-5E of VMFT-401 takes off from MCAS Yuma for another aggressor training mission.

(Jeremy Flack)

Not a new camouflage but one of the NATO tiger squadrons at a gathering.
(Jeremy Flack)

Variants

N-156: Two-seat trainer prototype.

N-156C: Single-seat prototype.

F-5A: Basic production fighter model.

F-5B: Two-seat trainer model of F-5A

F-5A-15: Similar to F-5A with uprated J-85-GE-15 engines.

CF-5A: Canadian built F-5A with uprated J85-CAN-15 engines and in flight refuelling capability.

CF-5D: Two-seat model of CF-5A

NF-5A: Canadian built variant with added Doppler navigation, manoeuvring flaps and larger drop tanks.

NF-5B: Two-seat trainer model of NF-5A.

RF-5A: Reconnaissance model of F-5A with modified nose.

F-5E: Enhanced model F-5A with uprated engines, wings and avionics.

F-5E (Saudi): F-5E with Litton LN-33 navigation system and

in flight refuelling capability.

RF-5E TigerEye: Reconnaissance model of F-5E with modified nose.

F-5F: Two-seat combat capable training model of F-5E.

F-5G Tigershark: Enhanced F-5E with single F404 engine and avionics upgrade. Subsequently redesignated F-20.

RF-5G: Norwegian air force designation for RF-5A.

SF-5A: Spanish built F-5A designated C-9 in service.

SF-5B: Spanish built F-5B designated CE-9 in service.

C-9: Spanish air force designation for SF-5A.

CE-9: Spanish air force designation for SF-5B.

F-20 Tigershark: Re-designated F-5G.

Above: Even the wing tip mounted AIM-9 Sidewinder was fully painted.

(Jeremy Flack)

Right: Cockpit of a Norwegian air force upgraded F-5A Freedom fighter.

(Jeremy Flack)

Index

Purchased for
the Buffalo
Library
by the
Buffalo
American
Legion